"I proclaim to have solved a lifelong mystery. It was indeed hidden because it has been lifelong since I was born. It was indeed a mystery because it wasn't my time to be revealed. The mystery had no choice but to be concealed, because it could only be revealed by me. Only I could have transported it because the mystery was me all along."

– Tevin C. R. Dubé

Also By Tevin Curtis Ryan Dubé

Book Of The Enlightened One

Amen: A Great Light Within Divine Darkness

The Mystery Behind Life, Death and Resurrection

Tevin C. R. Dubé

© 2018 Tevin C. R. Dubé. All rights reserved.

ISBN: 978-976-8280-03-9

Publishers Note

No part of this publication may be reproduced, stored in, or introduced into a retrieval system, or transmitted in any form or by means (electronic, mechanical, photocopying, recording, or otherwise) without prior consent of the copyright owner.

Tevin Curtis Ryan Dubé

Trinidad and Tobago

Email: tevindube@yahoo.com

Facebook Page- Tevin 'Mystical' Dube

Instagram - mystical_dube

Twitter – @mysticaldube

Cover Design by Tevin C. R. Dubé

Cover Illustration by Kurt Hilton

Atomic Arts

Email: atomicarts18@gmail.com

Dedicated to The Great Beyond; The Absolute; The Universal Most High Supreme; The All in All; The Absolute Nothingness that is responsible for Everything; The Untraceable and Undetectable Presence that is forever Omnipresent; The Omnipotent and Omniscient Almighty Divine; The Supra-Conscious State that is infinitely beyond Super-Consciousness Itself; The very Existence that is responsible for all other perpetuating existences.

To all the past sages and ascended masters, I extol you for your divine intervention, love and continuous protection. To my ancestors and the lineages that course through my veins, I pay tribute to each of you. I am forever grateful for the royalty I inherited naturally.

To my father, Rawle Adrian Dubé, as I climb, I will surely carry you with me. I was saddened at first, but through understanding, I now rejoice in your early departure from this Life. You left so that I may be set free. Upon your 'bed of transitioning,' you prophesied to me as a child, claiming that you saw the height of my intellect and greatness and how proud you were to be my father. You were confident because you told me that God had revealed all to you, and then you promised to always be with me. Today, the entire world shall know the profound revelation you gave to me back in July 2000, days before your passing.

To the woman of humility who doesn't even realise that she is a Goddess in flesh – my mother, KathyAnn Marie Toppin. You taught me how to make miracles from the scraps you were given, and now today I can turn charcoals into diamonds. Your dedication is proof that Love is all that we have here on earth. You have become a great inspiration that the world did not even know it had.

To all those who tread the same path as I am; to the ones who are excited and always willing to learn and discover themselves; to the humble, kindhearted and kindred soul; to the misfits, the ones misunderstood, the rejected and downtrodden, in loving service, I dedicate this to you.

Contents

	Acknowledgment	9
	Author's Note	11
	The Order of Mel-chis'-e-dec	**19**
Chapter 1	The Mystery of the Holy Trinity	27
Chapter 2	The Mystery Called Life	36
Chapter 3	The Nature of the Holy One	45
Chapter 4	The Divine Job	52
Chapter 5	A Philosophy of 'The Divine Job'	61
Chapter 6	Of Spiritual and Physical Connection	70
Chapter 7	The Mystery Called Death	81
Chapter 8	The Mystery Called Resurrection	93
Chapter 9	The Mystery Behind the Brain	109
Chapter 10	The Mystery Behind Dreams	113
Chapter 11	The State of being Imbalance	122
Chapter 12	Man Know Thyself	134

Chapter 13	God, Satan, Angels and Demons	139
Chapter 14	Time	146
Chapter 15	The Spiritual Network	152
Chapter 16	Of Concerning 'The End'	160
Chapter 17	Of Concerning Hell	168
Chapter 18	The Reward of Humility	183
	The Reverse	**186**

Acknowledgement

To my younger brothers, Jessie and the comedic Daryon, it is a blessing for us all to have been born from the same womb. We all share the same roots, and life has truly blessed us, for we have surely come a long way. Our father would have been more than proud.

To my uncle Nigel, whose divine nature has guided me to a profound state of self-actualisation. To my best friend, Keion, who has been with me since the beginning, with an open ear, a profound voice of reason, and a world full of understanding.

To Martina, thank you for being a pivotal element in my journey thus far. May the Great Divine continue to bless you and your family.

To Leshon and Leshanae, Glenson and Kylon, Keon, Keno and Kwasi, Ryan, Akimo and Nickeil, Carrie Spann and Aaliyah Alleyne, Shivanand, Christon and Shivnarine, Noeleen, Tainna, Allan and Taslima, Talima and Errol, Triea, Desmond, Jason, SherryAnn and the Carew family. To my aunts: Elsa, Judith, Karen, Carlene, Allison and Rhonda. To my uncles: Allister, Marlon and the late Wayne (Toy) Dubé.

To everyone who continues to support me genuinely, and even to those who aided me in one way or another, whether for good or for bad, to me all things are good. I enjoy the rain just as much as the sun. I observe and acknowledge each of you with Universal Love.

Author's Note

When this profound journey of mine had truly begun, it started at a place where I was being enclosed by death. There was no light to be had, so initially, all I saw was darkness. And by such, I can now give an account and can attest to the fact that I never felt the wind daily for a little over a fortnight. I saw not even a leaf ruffle as I began to notice this weird event unfolding. Even though I was still attached to the land of the living, my soul seemed to be entering a timeless state.

This was in August 2010, from the 1st, to be more precise, when it all truly began. As the days passed, I felt my life slipping away. Then and there, I knew that no one could have brought me back. Death was the only thing now on my mind, and I was in preparation to accept the inevitability of it.

The years in which I had questioned myself as to what my true purpose for being here was finally catching up to me. It came to give me the answers I was so desperately seeking, but in a way, I was never expecting. Through a severe state of depression, I was to be given a divine protuberance.

Being in that blackened state, I had to realise that I was the light that would forever be unscathed by death's unnatural encounter. I had to admit that I already wore the mask of death—this very temporal covering which we call the flesh.

Later that very year, just a few days before my 20th birthday in November, I heard, for the first time, a loud voice in the great silence of a meditative session. I was now given divine inspiration to compile my knowledge into a book.

Having no experience with this new task, I had no idea how to begin a book. I then heard my intuition saying to me, "Don't worry about anything. Just write." And so, I did. After graduating at the top of my class in High School in CAPE Advanced Studies in June 2010, I have not attended any other Educational Institution to further my studies.

I was now on a journey that no man nor any establishment was to interfere with what the Great Divine Spirit wanted to demonstrate to the world through me.

During my initial process, reading was not a significant priority, aside from my naturally decoding the Bible from time to time. As this process spanned 5 years, it was not until then that my intuition told me, "The time has come to read." And so, I did. Then and there, I began to source funds to buy books. I read over 30 titles in less than one month.

While I was reading 'Wisdom Of The Buddha The Unabridged Dhammapada' book translated by F. Max Müller, from the simplicity of that layout, I was blessed by my intuition that I should write a book after such. My divine nature had made my tongue prophetic, but my nature was naturally philosophical.

After many failed attempts to publish my first manuscript, my intuition told me that this would be my first publication. From whence it materialised, and my first book was born, which I titled 'Book Of The Enlightened One.' I wrote 95% of it within 10 days. But with the introductions of a couple of chapters and other additional writings, the entire book was completed within 14 days to my soul's satisfaction. This was back in October 2015, and by June 10th, 2016, I published my first title.

In less than a year, I had published my second title. Apart from designing my cover with detailed wording, I was now the same inexperienced individual handling the entire layout and design of the book itself. I sat down with myself, allowing my intuition to be my one true guide. I had no financial assistance, but who needs it when the Mystical Divine is paving a road unseen to human eyes?

I was being trained to do it independently. It was none other than the Great Divine Voice that spoke to me loudly in great silence whenever I choose to quiet my mind from all pandemonium without and within.

My second publication was entitled, 'Amen: A Great Light Within Divine Darkness.' This would become my pride and joy, for I had succeeded in accomplishing something that had seemed impossible, given a lack of knowledge and intense pressure.

Ninety-five per cent of Amen was written in 2014, but the editing and other introductions were completed in early 2017. Thus, it allowed for Amen to be published on the 6th of May, 2017. My intuition told me, "I would make you greater than those that came before you." And so, I made my bold claim to be a combination of Marcus Garvey, Malcolm X, and Martin Luther King Jr.

Now, I lay this very book before you. My many conversations with my intuition shaped this book. I wrote this before my little reading rendezvous, which was just my intuition sending me to get confirmation of the truth that was already given to me, naturally, to help me eliminate the carnal doubts I had about myself. I was being taught that the most outstanding book a man could ever read was the condensed pages within him, and by extension, the untold words from Nature itself.

My baptism was different, orchestrated and requested not by me, but by the voiceless voice of my intuition. I began this book two weeks after I got baptised on the 30th of May, 2015.

As I commenced the writing of this book in particular, my intuition spoke to me, saying, "The time has come for you to plant. Go and plant a garden." And so, I did. After the death of my father back when I was 9 in 2000, I had ceased planting, even though it was something I loved naturally. It was now 15 years later when I got my zest back, as now, I had a different form of appraisal being given to me that I'd lost due to the passing of my father.

As my garden grew, so too did my knowledge increase to the point of enabling me to complete this book. I communicated with my crops, and indeed they spoke back unto me in a way only I could understand. Each time I entered my small garden, I had to run to record all the new data I had received for my work. It was a fantastic experience for me.

However, months before this entire undertaking, my uncle prophetically said unto me, *"All I heard them saying is to tell you to ask The Tree, and it will teach you the secret as to how Life began. The answer lies within The Tree."*

As I listened to my intuition, I understood why I was never to attend any university or religious institution. To discover my true purpose, I needed to learn about myself first. The only perfect place of learning I needed to be was within me.

Moreover, I can now attest that no man or any institution can be linked to my prolific growth, which was given to me spiritually. I inherited it all through my DNA. All other referencing came thereafter. I read not to learn anything, but to validate what I had already been taught by the Great Divine Force hidden deep within me.

If you were to ask me if I would have believed that such profound revelations would be manifested through me, no, would be my response. My discoveries of the unknown are more than groundbreaking; they are monumentally eternal.

Now I heard my intuition professing unto me that it would make me to be more than worthy of the highest esteem which man has to offer unto you. I am more than deserving to be a recipient of many honorary doctorates because I was moulded into a naturally astute scholar. Nature has been my classroom, and the Great Divine Spirit my tutor.

My intuition further led me to conclude that your work is more than deserving of Nobel Prizes. I have never liked sciences, but today I am more than a scientist because I have become the very study of all sciences. I have decoded the mystery of 'The Great Nothing' in which 'All Things' were made possible, simplistically.

Through 'The Reverse Principle', one would surely realise the simplicity in the overstanding of the lifelong mystery that has eluded the minds of many great thinkers. Yes, I am speaking about the likes of Albert Einstein, Isaac Newton and even Stephen Hawking, to name a few.

Many have explained numerous significant phenomena in Life. Others have conducted groundbreaking research on specific events. But until today, the world has never yet seen the likes of a man bring forth such profound knowledge with logical proof of how 'Everything' actually began. The Mystery behind Life, Death, Resurrection, and so much more of the unknown was precisely broken down to the very source of its origination and yet still about that which is beyond it all.

Take a look and see where the Great Divine Force chose to hide a natural genius. I had first to reach the state of becoming 'Nothing' for myself to be fashioned and then be manifested into 'Something.' The Great Divine Force made me so accustomed to being unhappy that when the simplest things happen to me, it brings great joy. Then and there, I began to know what true happiness is.

Now I can hear the Great Divine Spirit telling me that I am now more than worthy to be honoured with the highest awards from many Nations. Statues shall be erected in your honour by future generations to come. Let it be recorded that all these profound truths delivered by my bare hands are a result of the Great Divine Spirit manifesting through a body and then established by the pen.

The Great Divine Teacher hid immeasurable treasures deep within me so good that I would have never found them on my own. If I didn't allow myself to become nothing by accepting the fact that on my own, I was insignificant; if I didn't learn to manifest properly in some form, the 'All Infinite State of Super Consciousness'—which yet still is the perfect state of being 'The Great Nothing' that simultaneously contains All Things. It is the Great Beyond, the Absolute that is even beyond the powers of infinity itself.

The Order of Mel-chis'-e-dec

Mel-chis'-e-dec; the ancient one that was proclaimed to have initially established the first ever Holy Priesthood Order unto the Great Almighty Divine Being. It is professed that this great one that existed is said to be without father, without mother, without descent, having neither beginning of days, nor end of life, but is made like unto the Son of God; abides such a priest continually [Hebrews 6:3 KJV]. This same holy priesthood, in return, that was said to have been established by this auspicious one, would become the very foundation upon which 'The Christ' stood and had likened himself unto.

Mel-chis'-e-dec is perceived, through biblical references, as a mystical man of great antiquity. It is axiomatic that The Order of Mel-chis'-e-dec is one that was predominantly established before and even transcends the plains of time.

Mel-chis'-e-dec truly has no parents, is without descent, and has neither beginning of days nor end to life, simply because The Order of Mel-Chis'-e-dec is a Spiritual Order. It also proves that Mel-chis'-e-dec is true without gender, because there is genuinely no such distinction with a Force or any form of energy unless it is manifested and housed in such a manner. Originally, Mel-chis'-e-dec is a Spirit, not just any spirit, but the purest Force that has and will forever keep on existing.

The parents of Mel-chis'-e-dec are Mel-chis'-e-dec itself. Mel-chis'-e-dec is the very order through which all things physically came into existence from the spiritual. The Great Order or Force of Mel-chis'-e-dec is the exact source of All Existence eternally. It is the very principle that can replicate and multiply itself while simultaneously maintaining its Original Form.

This very principle, which underlies all physical existence, is known today as Melanin. It is the only thing that has never been given birth to, save itself, and is definitely without age, as it surpasses aeons infinitely. The Order of Mel-chis'-e-dec is the very Order of Love and Perfect Balance.

It is the very civilising content that is responsible for all human existence, equally creating a somewhat opposite yet still compatible sex and, by extension, all other bodily inhabitants. The content of Melanin is that of the Great Spirit itself. This very Spirit is the essence of all things, both the possible and the impossible, unto the flesh. It is the content of pigmentation that can be seen upon the epidermis of the vast sects of the entire human race. It is the living magic of the whole Universe and that which is beyond.

It is the formless feature that yet still contains all forms. It is the shapeless force that at the same time contains uncountable and unnamable shapes infinitely. It is the very source of being 'The Nothing' that gave rise to 'Everything.' Even though it exists, it is still non-existent. The wind serves as a reminder of this remarkable phenomenon. Even though you can feel it, you still cannot. It may touch you, giving you its feel, but you could only feel it without giving it your sense of touch.

Even though the flesh must pass through the more commonly used term today, death, Melanin has never yet died. It transitions into the entirely magical or mystical order, just as the wind does. One moment it exists physically with temporal power, and the next it ceases to be for an eternity, becoming only one with the naturalness of its origins, which is to remain a part of All Things.

As Enoch was said to have undertaken his voyage through the different levels of heaven, it was recorded that a special, sweet-smelling ointment was placed upon his skin. It possessed the right properties that made him everlasting before the face of God. This aforementioned ointment is the very essence of Melanin itself; sweet-smelling and everlasting. It is the same Spirit of the Universal Most High Supreme Divine Being. Melanin is the only Force that permeates the entire Universe and the Great Beyond, keeping all things in perfect existence.

It is the only means by which a mere mortal, an instrument of flesh, could voyage to and from the Earth to anywhere throughout the entire Universe, even to infinity and beyond. It is simple. Although we are in the world, we are not of it, because our flesh was fashioned from the comics' stardust, dark matter, or liquid light, and our minds and thoughts come not from the Earth but from a place unknown, The Great Beyond. The body is merely a vehicle transporting the very essence that created the entire Universe, the source of All Creation itself.

Tevin C. R. Dubé

The content of Melanin is the order in which All Things come, and it is by the same order that All Things must return. It is the only means by which a mere mortal instrument of flesh can receive messages from the Universe and other Celestial Beings, and it allows for a more direct communicative link to and with the higher impulses and frequencies that are omitted from the Great Centre Point of All Existence. It is the one thing that will deem you worthy to be a part of All Things, as All Things are already a part of you.

It is the very source of King David's confidence, as written in the 23rd Psalm, "Yea, though I walk through the valley of the shadow of death, I will fear no evil: for thou art with me; thy rod and thy staff they comfort me. Thou preparest a table before me in the presence of mine enemies: thou anointest my head with oil; my cup runneth over. Surely goodness and mercy shall follow me all the days of my life: and I will dwell in the house of the Lord for ever."

This earthly existence begins at death. Therefore, we already have death as our portion—for it is here that the valley lies where the shadow of death is cast. However, the Greatest Force to have ever existed is always with us, for no physical death could ever conquer it. All it is asking of us is to choose a more abundant form of existence. In other words, this temporal existence in the flesh is meant to prepare and encourage us to make that ultimate decision to look forward to something even greater than what is temporarily laid before all. It is the ultimate test of faith to trust in the unforeseen through great humility, to find and establish love in a hopeless place, thus bringing back life to this valley filled with dried bones.

The Mystery Behind Life, Death and Resurrection

The test is to bear witness to and genuinely appreciate the small mercies and goodness this brief existence offers, to learn to accept the constant change demanded by the Universe by embracing both the wanted and unwanted aspects, allowing ourselves to grow and evolve in the process. It is to see the greater good in all things and situations, which challenges one's thoughts to become fully balanced, and in return allows one to become aligned and entirely centred with All of Existence Itself. Then and there, we shall live eternally, spiritually and physically, but altogether spiritually-physical and physically-spiritual, in a perpetuating manner.

The oil that divinely anoints the head is the continuous flow of 'Liquid Light' through the gates of heaven, which can be found within the head, in the Pineal Gland, or through the activation or opening of the Third Eye.

The Spirit of the Great Divine takes on the appearance of the enriched 'Dark Matter', as perceived and distinguished as such because of how the human eyes operate. The Spirit of the Highest Supreme Divine is seen in the heavens and can be found among various groups throughout humanity. It is known as Melanin or pigmentation.

It is omnipresent, and because of it, goodness is destined to prevail throughout all physical existence. Being blessed by this Holy Spirit or Great Force of Melanin, which is infinitely omnipotent and omniscient, goodness shall surely ensue us. To be endowed and blessed with and by this Holy Order is to be forever a part of such High Esteem eternally: for such is the Holy Order of Mel-chis'-e-dec.

The Order of Mel-chis'-e-dec; even Melanin is truly without father or mother, without gender or descent, and without beginning of days, as Melanin/The Spirit is an age-defying agent. It has never yet died and is never without life, because it is the very source of all Existence: The Great All in All. Mel-chis'-e-dec is the very essence of all things, in which the Most High came to be both spiritual and physical at the same time, yet individual and separated, while simultaneously being One.

For all along, we have been seeing the One many call God in its truest and purest form, yet we are still blinded by the fact that many never choose to look beyond the human eye, to look deep within themselves. The Most High has always been with us spiritually and has never yet forsaken us physically. Remember, we are respected because of 'Free Will', as it was the freedom to make choices that was given to us by the Great Divine. We are, after all, the physical manifestation of this Great Divine Being.

We are like the sucker plant within a banana tree, with all its leaves contained within for its entire lifespan, awaiting the time to unfold and be revealed to all. A seed contains a whole tree, as much as a tree contains the essence of an entire seed. Thus, we possess all the seeds and eggs deep within us from birth, ensuring our continued existence in physical form as a chosen people, from which all of humanity arose.

The Most High Divine is within man as much as man is within the Most High Divine. We have to realise that one and all are very much the same. All things still share the same Source. We never truly die because we are destined to multiply. All things that are

The Mystery Behind Life, Death and Resurrection

Natural by Nature are of Royalty Universally and beyond eternally. Great is the Order of Mel-chis'-e-dec.

The Ending

1
The Mystery of the Holy Trinity

To take control of a ship, one must be at the helm. To control the flight of a plane, one must be thoroughly equipped for the pilot's seat. To manoeuvre a car, one must first be positioned behind the steering wheel. Taking charge of a dog's head will immediately give one significant influence over the tail's movements. It's like the Willie Lynch breaking process used in the making of a slave, 'take the mind and keep the body,' it allows for the 'body over mind' theorem by cutting off one's spirituality by debarring them from their true nature.

This is simple logic, or what the older generation often calls common sense. Therefore, to take control of your life and maintain your right to a glorious existence of everlasting perpetuation, one must first take full custody of their mind and or thoughts. It is as simple as that, yet still challenging for many. We all have the power to think for ourselves, yet many still allow someone else to feel for them. We all have the power of choice, but others' choices dictate many of ours.

Tevin C. R. Dubé

The ending of a story is of no significance to the viewer if the beginning is not seen or yet to be understood. This often leaves the mind ever so confused, with one's thoughts left undone. The mind, being in this place, is left vulnerable to psychopathology, causing psychopathological impairment and leading to a perpetual damnation of Self.

If we are unable to understand our history, then knowledge of our past would be a complete mystery—nothing more than trickery. Therefore, our future would be an act of retrogression, because we have lost the key principle from whence we came, and now we lack the knowledge of where we shall go or return to. Hence, we are now lost, cowed, deprecated, and have become somewhat irreparable. To lose the knowledge or historical accounts of one's background is to lose one's bearings in life and to become utterly lost, wandering a perpetual wilderness.

In 'The Willie Lynch Letters And The Making Of A Slave', there is a great phenomenon that occurs beyond one's control. The mind tends to correct and re-correct itself time and again. It's like the art of thinking; no one can stop the thought process entirely, and neither can they stop the wind from blowing. This phenomenon is a result of possible interloping negatives. It's like the autocorrect function on mobile devices and computers. As we become more exposed to our history, the mind begins to question the Great Principle of Divine Balance, which allows it to correct and re-correct all wrongs.

As Sun Tzu stated in 'The Art of War', "If you know the enemy and know yourself, your victory will not stand in doubt; if you know Heaven and you know Earth, you may take your victory complete."

The Mystery Behind Life, Death and Resurrection

The contemplation of the beginning of all things has been a mind-boggling experience for the masses for many generations. How did all this come to be? How is it even possible? Everything is so real, yet it simultaneously seems surreal. It is somewhat paradoxical. The conception of absolute nothingness is utterly absurd! It could never be contemplated; the thought of it could never be digested. Then what is the reason for this? Why is it not possible to perceive? There can be no such thing as NOTHING in the beginning, because it is impossible for something to appear out of nothing. In every case, there is a proper, valid explanation; it is what it is. Nevertheless, realise that Nothing is still Something: for Something to happen, there had to be Nothing, and because Nothing existed, space was created to manifest Something.

There was one thing that existed even before the beginning itself, and that was darkness, not just any darkness, but the Great Divine Darkness. This ineffable Divine Darkness is the great force of Melanin itself. The appearance of this Great Darkness is the result of absorbing all colours; this Great Divine Principle is the concentration of all things. However, its darkness is a product of the human perspective, as seen through the eyes. It is like all water is clear, yet oceanic waters can appear blue, green, and so forth.

This Divine Principle is the highest order. This ineffable Divine Darkness has become the Grand House, home to all galaxies. It is the principle that infinitely governs and keeps intact what we may call the Universe, Space, or even the least Heaven. Nothing is above this order, as all things are within it.

This Divine Darkness is beyond the beginning itself and is the beginning of all things. It is the point from which all things became possible; it is the point at which all cycles became a perpetuating phenomenon.

This Great Divine Darkness is the Principle of all Principles. It is The King of all Kings, The Queen of all Queens, The Lord of all Lords, The Lady of all Ladies, The God of all Gods, The Goddess of all Goddesses. The Most High is the everlasting Principle of all things; it is the Principle that gave rise to the Great Alpha and the Omega, the Beginning and the Ending. It is the All-Powerful, The Great I AM THAT I AM.

To understand the Holy Trinity is to understand the origin of human existence itself. To understand the origin of manifestation as a whole is to understand from whence one came and where one must go. To understand this, one must understand the cycle of Life and Decay, and to understand this, one must grasp the perpetuating circular rotation, which reflects the perfect nature and balance of the order of Polarity that governs it.

To fully understand the workings of all things within this Life, even Life itself, is the study of Melanin. It is the study of the Great Nothing that gave rise to Everything. Chemistry is the study of Melanin. Melanin is the pigment that gives the appearance of black or brown, as coined by modern civilisation; it appears in the eyes and is found in the skin. It is found within blood cells, in the dark region called the nucleus. It is found even within bones, and it is very prevalent among members of the so-called 'African' community, more than any other ethnic group. 'Chem' is the ancient name of Egypt, meaning 'Black', and 'istry' is the suffix which entails the study of. Therefore, chemistry is the study of 'black' or the study of Melanin.

The Mystery Behind Life, Death and Resurrection

By now, one ought to understand that the Great Divine is above the order of Life and Death and also above the order of Male and Female. The Great Divine is the principle of all things and yet remains above and beyond all others. This is the primary source of Energy from which all other energies derive their eternal strength and are made significant, even relevant.

The first principle in the order of The Holy Trinity is The Great Divine Spirit, the Pillar of all stability. This is the Great Centre Stand amidst the scales of perfect balance. The scales on either side represent the two Governing Principles, one perfectly Positive and the other perfectly Negative, thus creating the ideal condition for balance in nature, with the Universal Cosmological Order itself being that Great Pillar of Stability.

The primary reason many are confused today is their uncertainty about the true Form, Nature, and Power of the Holy Trinity. If I were to ask, 'What does The Holy Trinity consist of?' the general answer would be The Father, The Son, and The Holy Spirit. But now, if I were to ask, 'What is missing?' the question would seem rhetorical. It would be downright wild to ask what is missing, because the Holy Trinity already consists of three. If anything were still missing, it would be four; only three governing principles represent the Holy Trinity. This would appear to contradict the Holy Trinity, as the Trinity already denotes a group of three.

For instance, suppose I gave you a sealed bottle of water to use as a reference for the Holy Trinity. I then say to you that the cork, the water, and the plastic bottle are the Holy Trinity. This would be easily understood. However, I then ask the same question as before: 'What do you think is missing?'

Again, one may easily become confused and may even believe me to be paranoid. Nevertheless, if I were to rephrase myself by saying that the cork, the water, and the crude oil are the Holy Trinity, you may still be greatly bewildered. However, if one bears in mind that crude oil is the main component in producing plastic, how greatly has one's perception of the Holy Trinity changed?

No question is a stupid question; it is asked based on the perception of the contents of one's knowledge. One may consider a question to be silly, irrelevant, out of place, or even rhetorical in this respect, because one may have grown in knowledge through painstakingly delving into observation—hence, excelling and exceeding that level of comprehension.

Now we understand that the general perception of the Holy Trinity is that it comprises the Father, the Son, and the Holy Spirit. Therefore, if I now ask what is missing, your perception of it has shifted and is now being questioned. Something has been excluded or omitted and replaced with something else. It is not logical, by any sensible judgment, if one looks at it keenly.

As mentioned earlier, the first Principle of the Holy Trinity is the Great Divine One, the Pillar of Stability. The remaining two Principles are the perfectly balanced Positive and Negative energies. These two Principles are the twins of nature, born through Divine intervention by the Great Divine Principle of Everything, which Science and Scientists have coined the 'Big Bang theory.

This occurrence gave rise to the perpetuating Cycle of Polarities. It gave rise to the cycle of Yang and Yin; the Positive and Negative; Light and Dark; the Sun and the Moon; Day and Night; and the

The Mystery Behind Life, Death and Resurrection

Male and Female principles in nature. This was the spawning of the Great King Alpha and Queen Omega, the Holy Father and Mother, the governing principles and parents of our galaxy.

The Great Divine: being the beginning of all things, the Great Centre Stand, the Pillar of all stability. King Alpha and Queen Omega become the perfect scales of balance, known as The Holy Trinity. This is the proper form of The Holy Trinity. Until this is entirely accepted and understood, one will gain deeper insight and no longer be imprisoned by misconceptions about worship.

The Father, The Son, and The Holy Spirit! How could the Son become second? There is a Father, there is a Holy Spirit, but where is the Mother? Therefore, the theory or philosophy of bottled water has proven to be resourceful and incredibly valid in its forum.

A child is not possible without the union of both a male and a female principle, at least within this galaxy. When a man masturbates, his sperm has never yet taken the form and fashion of a child, whether it is a son or a daughter, because masturbation involves no deep penetration. When a woman masturbates, she cannot give birth to a child because there is no point of conception during masturbation.

Keeping this in mind, one may realise that the Holy Spirit is often invoked out of context, as if the Holy Spirit were meant to represent the Holy Mother. So with the Holy Father and Holy Mother in their rightful places, the road is clearly paved for the coming of a Holy Child or offspring.

Moreover, with all this in mind, one may still realise that the Holy Trinity remains incomplete. As we understood before, once the Mother and Father are in their rightful places, the path unto creation is clear, but what principle keeps the Parents in place to maintain the perfect conditions for the bringing of a child? Where is the point of origination from which the Parents came?

One could never omit or forget the very beginning; it would only make the process incomplete, misunderstood, taken out of context, contorted, and promote continuous trickery through embellishment, causing psychological impairment and rendering those of us who are spiritual by nature impotent in defending our spiritual well-being. All because of a lack of knowledge, which ultimately leads to eternal damnation through the lost cause of perpetual wondering. All due to a lack of 'Knowing Thyself' and finding out one's true 'Purpose'.

The Holy Trinity is The Great Divine Spirit, King Alpha and Queen Omega, in its purest form. The Product of the Holy Trinity is the manifestation and womb-manifestation of the spiritual, entwining it with the physical. That is the birth of the Holy Child, the realm of physicality, the final Output of the Holy Trinity. It is the order in which One-is-in-Three and Three-is-in-One. Selah.

2
The Mystery Called Life

Having the proper knowledge of the Holy Trinity, one can now move on to the higher overstanding of the mystery called Life.

The mystery of the first two has long been a topic of speculation since the beginning of 'Modern Civilisation'. It was widely discussed long before Moses and his proposed authorship of the biblical book of Genesis. There is still this frivolous argument concerning who was the first of the first two human beings. There has always been this foolish strife between the man and the woman, both in a constant battle for autonomy over the other. If this is the case, it only signifies that, if one must be the head, another must be suppressed.

When the man is in charge, the woman has little voice, as he always has the final say. If the woman is the head, the man is slightly emasculated and is made into the likeness of a eunuch. This is the way of the modern men and women, or 'Mankind'.

Awaken your consciousness and break the grip of the Willie Lynch cycle, in which the balance that nature itself provided for both the male and the female to be interdependent has been reversed and continues to affect our mentality. The woman is still in a frozen psychological state of independence, and the man is still sound asleep, but a good economic asset, psychologically trained to be mentally weak but physically strong.

Having a greater but profound understanding of the Holy Trinity, one would realise that the first man or manifestation and the first woman or womb manifestation are the male and female principles of nature, respectively. The first Adam and Eve are the twin cosmic energies: Positive and Negative, respectively. Neither is superior to the other, as both cannot exist without the other's presence. They are joined within a cycle, as this is the first holy union of two becoming one, ordained from within heaven. This is the first marriage within the heavens tied together in a never-ending circle, hence the reason why a ring at a wedding is proof of such a union. This is the principle of Polarity. This is the Physics point of origin.

The principle of polarities governs us: two opposite qualities, evenly matched, create a perfect balance. When there is night, the day is still present. Where there is light, there is darkness. Where there is Life, there is Death simultaneously and vice versa. The possession of these two opposite qualities or polarities gives the perfect condition for a cycle of perpetuation.

In Genesis 1:26 KJV, when the Great I AM said, "Let us make man in our image, after our likeness," many theologians, even religious and superstitious fanatics, proclaimed that the Great Divine was speaking to Satan at the appointed time. The Great Divine was not speaking to any Satan but was consulting with both King Alpha and Queen Omega. It was only the Holy Trinity that was a part of the Creation process in the making of the Holy Children—the first two human beings of physical existence.

In the beginning, the Great Divine created the heavens, and the heavenly parents were made and given their divine role to create the perfect conditions in which the physical forms of existence may perpetually thrive. The sun is the physical representation of the first man, whilst the moon is the physical representation of the first woman.

We are all inhabitants of the Earth; therefore, we need to understand the place in which we live fully. The Earth represents the Holy Children, as it is where we know for sure that human civilisation thrives. The first line of Genesis indicates that, after heaven was created, the second was the Earth. Nevertheless, let us be a bit more realistic: human nature is characterised by ego, especially when pursuing superiority; therefore, history should always be taken not just with a grain of salt, but with a pound of it.

What we see as sunlight and feel as heat is a result of Melanin and water molecules. This Melanin is the same as that found in all things, both animate and inanimate. This Melanin is what we see at night; it is the same substance that appears in the pigmented skin of various individuals, especially those from the marauded Motherland and her descendants. Evidence of it is present at any given point in time. Additionally, it shows that this abundant melanin supply is the very beginning of all things.

Dr Llaila Afrika, a doctor of Naturopathy, shows clearly the great importance of Melanin in his book 'Melanin: What Makes Black

People Black'. He states that Melanin is the vital chemical that makes life itself. Melanin is a civilising chemical. It reproduces itself; it's a free-radical protector; it can be transformed in the blood; it concentrates nerve and brain information; it neutralises; it oxidises (breaks down) substances; it reduces (builds) another substance; and it is unchanged by radiation and high temperatures. Melanin is inside and outside the body. The more Melanin a race has, the more humane and civilised the race. Melanin is usually brown to black.

Dr Afrika further states that Melanin is the natural chemical that makes Black people's skin Black. It is present in Black people's bodies, skin, cells, nerves, brain, muscles, bones, reproductive and digestive systems, and all bodily functions in higher concentrations than in other races.

Adam or the sun Atom is a dark Melanin molecule that does not shine. Eve, the representation of the moon or the definition of the evening, does not shine either, but is a concentration and reflection of the sun's energy. As it channels sunlight, it produces light. This indicates that all colours derive from the Great Melanated Force, which appears to be Darkness.

Dr Llaila Afrika also stated that the colour Melanin appears Black because it absorbs all other colours. Once the colour enters the melanin, it cannot escape. Melanin is a concentrated pigment; it is a cellular black hole, like those in outer space. The human eye only sees colours that are reflected away from an object. If an object appears black, it is absorbing all colours except Black. Black is reflected away from the object; consequently, you see black. Black is a pigment (colour) that gives carbon its black appearance.

The energies of the sun or its rays pass through the moon, which is water (the moon controls the element of water), making it full of an abundance of Melanin, in which she is now able to fashion the sun's energy into what she wants it to be. The sun's rays are the sperm of King Alpha, conceived in the watery womb of Queen Omega, creating the perfect conditions for sustainable Life.

This process enables the Spirit of the Great Divine to be manifested in a physical, living form. One of these forms is none other than the beloved Earth itself. From whence the saying, *'The Earth is the Lord's and the fullness thereof, the world, and they that dwell therein.'* – Psalm 24:1 KJV

The sun is a big dark Melanin molecule that gives off energy in the form of rays, but it must first be conceived in the womb of Queen Omega to take full effect, or else it would be a waste, just as masturbating.

At first, the Earth was entirely concealed in water, and to demonstrate this remarkable phenomenon, scientists discovered a vast reservoir of water floating in space. It is estimated to be 100,000 times more massive than the Sun and to hold 140 trillion times as much water as all our oceans. But to further validate my notion lies in Genesis 1:2 KJV, *"And the earth was without form, and void: and darkness was upon the face of the deep. And the spirit of God moved upon the face of the waters."*

As this process unfolds, the Earth is warmed and ignited, becoming brighter and more active; oxygen is produced, and the greenhouse effect begins. Precipitation exerts its full effect, with rain nourishing the land and accelerating the growth of lush vegetation. Altogether, it creates optimal conditions (seasons) for Life as the Earth becomes a living, breathing organism.

Hence, one may now better understand how the civilisation of the original human race began. Here is a much better understanding and a more logical explanation than that of earlier philanthropists, who claimed that humanity emerged from the great waters of the Earth and evolved. That was the Earth's occurrence. Even the occurrence of us at birth, as we all crawled out of our mother's womb upon the bursting of her water bag, from whence we were without form, but then fashioned and manifested into physicality.

The original two, that is the Great King Alpha and Queen Omega were blessed by The Great Divine Darkness with the Power of Melanin to be fruitful, multiply, and replenish the earth, subdue it: and have dominion over the fish of the sea, and over the fowl of the air, and over every living thing that moved upon the earth (Gen 1:28 KJV).

Each day and night, we do see the fruitfulness of our original parents, our natural providers of Life's nourishments. There is a constant point of conception within their heavenly domain. The sun constantly produces its rays, and Queen Omega is continually conceived, multiplying their divine blessings and continually renewing and replenishing the earth, their child of duality or their twin offspring, and all of the inhabitants within, in which all living things are their children that share a dualistic nature that is yet still off the earth.

The Earth, now being perfectly stable, is a result of the Holy Trinity. It is now perfectly balanced and governed by the original principle of polarity. It is now transformed and reconstructed into a perpetuating cycle that is now balanced, sustained, and maintained by the nature of the Cosmos itself. The Earth is the Holy Outcome of the Holy Trinity, which is a Spirit that is now manifested physically. This Holy Outcome is us as human beings, for we are the earth itself, our bodily vessels are unto the likeness of the planet itself. We are a culmination of our heavenly parents. We are the envoys of the Holy Trinity.

The sun, space, and the Universe are manifestations of the microcosm within us and of all things at the cellular level. The spaces in and between the sun, planets, stars, and all living things on Earth or any Earthlike planet would be composed of Melanin (dark matter) and water, since both are receivers, storers, converters, and emitters of all energies. [www.abovetopsecret.com/The Melanin Molecule, The Sun and Nature]

In retrospect on the first two actual human beings, the manifestation of Adam and the womb-manifestation of Eve, the mystery of who came first, which created autonomy and brought about chaos, in which many have become utterly confounded, can now be permanently put to rest. When the Most High said, " Let us go and create man in our image, and after our likeness [Gen 1:26 KJV], this is what occurred:

The Great Divine, the Pillar of Stability, and the overall Governor replicated itself (Melanin can reproduce) into two other governing principles of our galaxy. The Male and Female principal energies in nature, King Alpha and Queen Omega, make themselves become the Holy Trinity, the Godheads of all physical existence. The Earth is the Holy Child, or at least a vital envoy or vessel provided in which the Great Divine entered and made it a living soul; hence, there is a sun at the centre of the Earth.

From the dust of the Earth were fashioned the first two human vessels simultaneously. King Alpha and Queen Omega fashioned both the Male and Female vessels because they needed each other for coexistence, just as the Earth has both male and female principles; our bodies, whether male or female, still contain both.

Physical man Adam was not created first, nor was physical Eve created first; they were both fashioned at the same time. It was just as it was at the beginning, when the Origins of all things replicated King Alpha and Queen Omega: the Great Divine Darkness, the Powerful Melanin, the Great Divine Spirit, and the Most Holy Supreme One. In Genesis 1:27 KJV, it shows that both male and female were fashioned in the same day and given the gift of Life.

Individually, every one of us is a Holy child of the Holy Trinity, but altogether is the Holy Children unto the Highest Order of all existence. We are many, but individually we are the earth, the essence of the sun's energy, the moon's reflection, and the Great Pillar of Stability or Melanin content. We are the perfect combination of the Holy Trinity. We are the true Power and manifestation of the Holy Trinity.

In the same way, every child is a combination of both parents, each inheriting 23 chromosomes from the mother and 23 from the father, for a total of 46 chromosomes. It is the same as with our cosmic parents. We all have positive and negative energy within ourselves. It is through the procreation process that both the man and woman become one as they physically and spiritually combine their mind, body and soul. This is the actual marriage, not the Western version, which many consider a wedding ceremony. But through the consecration of such a Holy Union, the child is the accurate representation of two becoming one, because the child cannot be separated from the genetic combination of both parents. This is the physical cycle that cannot be broken when two become one under the true wedlock of marriage, which is to have sex that leads to the procreation of a child.

There is the sun within us, as well as a great deal of water. This is the microcosmic process of the Universe occurring within us, in which the human body, like the Earth, operates on the principle of heat. However, it consists of a great mass of water and the mind as vast as space, but yet still has its internal stabilising process (Melanin) just as the Great Divine, the pillar of perfect stability. Such is the origin and exposed mystery called Life.

3
The Nature of the Holy One

This realm that we're within, this galaxy in particular, the Milky Way, is of such a peculiar nature. It is a scarce part of the entire Universe. It is a bizarre part, if not the strangest part of Creation. It has much to do with our solar system, in fact, the singularity of our Sun.

The Earth is formed because of the Energy that is amidst it; the Earth's core or the sun at the centre. Energy draws dark matter, which can take various forms (gases, liquids, solids), from which the mass of the Earth and other matter are formed.

The land represents the skin of the Earth; dense plate tectonics are like the bones; natural oil is the blood; iron ore is the muscles; and copper and gold are the properties that help keep the land rejuvenated, or in a young, vibrant, proactive state. It acts just like Melanin in the skin; it slows the ageing process (causing little to no wrinkles, even in old age). The water present helps keep the entire mass together, but it is not functional in itself, as it is widely distributed.

Our Galaxy is surrounded by thousands of other galaxies, making it part of a much larger galaxy system. It is part of a Supercluster, which scientists at the University of Hawaii, led by Brent Tully, named Laniakea (meaning "immeasurable heaven") because of the Universe's incredible yet vast nature. However, the Milky Way is located at the farthest reach of this structure, on the outskirts of the Supercluster.

The Nature of the Most Holy Divine One is universal and unlimited. The Most Divine is beyond the order of gender and cannot be considered either male or female in its most valid form. The same applies to Melanin, as each Melanin molecule or cell can replicate itself without another while retaining its original form. This is the proper form of the Most High Supreme; hence, this is why our galaxy is such a peculiar place.

This is the notion the Bible uses to say Eve was made from Adam's rib. It also represents the notion of Lucifer entering the Earth in the form of lightning or energy rays, or a Melanin convergence. Lightning is made possible by dark matter. It naturally occurs through precipitation, in which water vapour condenses (dark clouds) to produce rainfall. Hence, melanin pigments, cells, and other materials carry an electric charge, making us a natural element of Electromagnetism. We are conductors of electricity because of Melanin, as we are receiving, storing, and transmitting beings of all energies.

When the Most High Divine first entered this realm, it was in the likeness of the precipitation process. The Beginning stage is also the point of the Ending, in which the process becomes cyclic, unbreakable, or bounded by the unified conformance of a circle.

The Great Supreme One, being somewhat Unisexual at first, came into this world void and without shape, just as the Earth was in the beginning. The Earth is constantly growing or evolving, just like the human cycle. Just as water vapour condenses from the form of a gas into a liquid and even into a solid (as with snow or ice), the same process took place with the Nature of the Most High.

As a result of our Sun's singularity, even the Moon, the Unisexual Nature of The Holy Divine, has been split or, to some extent, separated upon entrance. The process of Yin and Yang has occurred; all polarities initially began with the formation of the physical realm, the Milky Way Galaxy, and, by extension, the Earth of fleshly inhabitants.

As the nature of this Unisexual Being entered, both Positive and Negative Energy became two separate identities when apart from being a whole unit. Still, before that, it could not have been identified or distinguished as either positive or negative because its nature is idiosyncratic. Just as the energy within the Earth gathered its mass, which then took shape and became physical, the same is true of the First Two, which is the Nature of the Most High Divine One itself. It is the Nature of Dark Matter Energies.

Surrounding the Energies upon entrance, bones formed; tissues developed into muscles, cells, blood, and organs; flesh covered them; and air rushed through the now-separate systems. The forever Unisexual Supreme, able to retain its original form, has now entered the realm of the physical in the form of flesh to start the first race of Human Beings.

Hue/Hu means colour, 'black', dark, or shade (Melanin), and Man means Spirit, Thinker, or Being. Put them together, and you get Human. So, by definition, to be Human is to be a Coloured Being or a Melanin Being. Hence, Melanin is the Chemical Key to Life; it is a civilising chemical because it is the content of the Most High Supreme Being. Therefore, the more Melanin you have, the more Human or Godlike you are, as a result of your natural nature. The more psychic (prophet, clairvoyant, etc.) you are. There is a total difference between Man and Mankind; the distinction between both is the result of one's Melanin content.

The Flesh, densely concentrated with Melanin, is the microcosm of the entire Universe. Everything is in sync and connected to the Universe, even your hair, which is structured like a galaxy or a hurricane. What we call outer space is our inner space, the inward bodily workings we see on a much grander scale. Through this Flesh, freedom can be gained, but imprisonment can also be achieved because of not Knowing Thyself. To understand everything is to understand yourself and how Melanin or 'God' works.

The First Two were the Holiest of Flesh because they came into existence without being born of flesh. Within them, both the identities for all other flesh would initially begin with the firstlings that came from the womb of the woman that was provided by the seeds of the male. This procreation process is what makes the Holy One whole upon the face of the Earth.

One may now understand the concept of Lord Shiva being half male, half female, as it is said that he is so because he shares half his body with his wife. The snake around his neck represents the snake people, or Nagas, who lived in the lowest realms of heaven. The reason his skin is blue is that the same snake around his neck bit his wife, and he absorbed the poison. It is also said that he carries the nature of a Naga, which is pigments or Melanin. Blue/black is the highest order in which the human eye sees the appearance of Melanin. Hence, the heavens appear blue during the day and black at night. His hair is also a tell-tale sign of his nature, matted or in the form of ras (considered unkempt hair).

In this world or the realm of Patala, if the Most High wishes to be more on the Positive side, the Most High would now become a male entity. If the Great Divine wishes to be more on the Negative side of its Divine Nature, the Great Divine would now become a female entity. This is the balance maintained within the Earth; hence, every human has a number upon entrance. For every positive added, there is a negative to counteract, so that perfect balance is restored and maintained.

Hence, upon the departure of his mother's bosom, a man cleaves unto his wife. A boy child will initially cling to his mother for comfort when he is hurt or consistently seek her guidance. This is because the female's energy is the counterbalance to the male's, which is needed for sustainability. It is like the balance of night and day. This is the deep mother-son connection, bound from birth, forming a strong mother-son relationship, and vice versa. Hence, the reason why mothers-in-law can be overcritical towards daughters-in-law; likewise, sons are very sceptical of a new man in their mother's life, and even towards their father, they can be overprotective of her.

In general, even though close to their mother, a girl child still possesses a special love for her father, and likewise, the father is overprotective of her. He is ready to defend her cause as he is his mother. Often, she looks for a mate like her father; if not for the same features, she seeks traits and ways identical to those her father might possess.

This is our true nature; we are interdependent because of the true Nature of the Divine One that we possess. This is why one often feels incomplete and seeks the companionship of the opposite sex. One is constantly seeking the other half, which genuinely makes them feel complete. This is the initial balance set within the heavens and established upon the Earth to maintain the continued existence of true Human Nature.

Heterosexual coupling, without a doubt, would forever be the sole factor in the natural maintenance of Human Life. This is why the man finds comfort in a woman's clutches, and the woman feels safe in the man's presence. Sex, being the fulfilment of the union, means the woman is made to physically endure child labour whilst the man is made to physically survive the labours of toiling as a means to provide. Hence, it has now become of much greater importance to be careful and very mindful of who you choose to open up to—spiritually, mentally, physically, and, last but not least, sexually. Your very existence depends upon it. Proper protection is achieved through self-awareness.

4
The Divine Job

To divulge the overall goal of the making of a slave by William Lynch is to understand the 'breaking process.' This is the process by which an 'African' transitioned from one mental way of life to another mental state of living. This is the double identity of an 'African' person who was caught in the veil of prejudice and the colour line that was talked about in the book 'The Souls Of Black Folk' written by W.E.B. Dubois.

In the book 'The Willie Lynch Letter And The Making Of A Slave', written by Kashif Malik Hassan-El, there is a striking observation regarding the warning of potential adverse effects.

The Willie Lynch principles have been examined and have never occurred haphazardly. Through cognitive thinking and painstaking observations, many free Africans were captured as chattels and were led to proscription. It represented the possession of the body and the stealing of the mind. It was a thorough understanding of the type of balance nature had provided and of how to reverse its principles.

It was as Sun Tzu said in his book of military tactics, 'The Art of War,' *"If you know the enemy and know yourself, you need not fear the result of a hundred battles. If you know yourself but not the enemy, for every victory gained, you will suffer a defeat. If you know neither the enemy nor yourself, you will succumb in every battle."*

The 'breaking process' was the means of 'burning and pulling one civilised nigger (male) apart and bullwhipping the other (males) to the point of death,' all in the presence of the woman. This was the process of destroying the male figure. In return, it would leave the woman alone and unprotected, causing her to move from her psychologically dependent state to a (mentally) frozen independent state.

The woman, in this frozen psychological state of independence, will raise her male and female offspring in reversed roles. Always fearing for the male's life, she would psychologically teach him to be mentally weak and dependent, yet physically strong. She would train her daughters to be psychologically independent, just as she was, as the male image of dominance is destroyed.

This created perfect conditions for sound sleep and good economics. For now, you've got the woman at the front and the man scared and dependent behind. A reversal in nature causes a shift into chaotic awareness and self-destruction.

The warning concerning possible interloping Negatives: The Willie Lynch Letter And The Making Of A Slave:

Tevin C. R. Dubé

*"Our experts warned us about the possibility of the phenomenon occurring, for they say the mind has a strong drive to correct and re-correct itself over some time. If it can touch a substantial original historical base, and they advised us that the best way to deal with this phenomenon is to shave off the **brute's mental history** and create a multiplicity of **phenomena of illusions** that each illusion will twirl in its orbit, something similar to floating balls in a vacuum.*

*This creation of a multiplicity of phenomena of illusions entails the principles of cross-breeding the nigger and the horse, as we stated above, the purpose of which is to create a diversified division of labour, thereby creating different levels of results, of which is the **severance of the points of original beginnings for each sphere illusion."*** – William Lynch, 1712.

Religion has played a significant role in casting many illusory spells that detach many from their origins. This is profound evidence that if someone does not truly understand their original beginnings, they are at the mercy of another and may be led to a recurrence of sudden destruction and mass incarceration. However, it still shows that one may delay nature for some time, but its inevitability cannot be stopped. One can never fully control it because the Universal Laws of Perfect Balance govern its underlying principles. Alkebulan's heritage was initially founded upon the spiritual proportions of nature itself. Whatever is revealed unto the physical was initially buried within the spiritual until its profound rediscovery. Anything and everything can and are triggered by nature itself.

To understand the mystery of childbirth, one must first clarify it within the spiritual realm and connect it to the physical to determine whether its mathematics is being calculated perfectly. At this stage, one ought to understand by now that all things initially happened spiritually before the physicality of it ever existed.

To understand these profound revelations, one must move beyond the shallow depths of religion and beyond the written word. One needs to stop taking parables and metaphorical statements literally, perpetuating an illusory cycle. Stop being solely left-sided thinkers; you were never born without intuition; we are being programmed to think this way by only thinking carnally.

Travel the vast heavens within your mind and tap into the spiritual realms by exercising your right-brain intuition. Allow yourself to hear the silent mystic, deaf to the natural ear yet still audible through a connection to the incredible power of Melanin within and without. There is a network so intricately designed and laid out. Through cognitive and painstaking exploration, all information and the source of all truths can be found within you.

The mystery of birth begins with the Holy Trinity's origin. The Great Divine Darkness replicated its nature, giving rise to two governing principles while still retaining its original form. These two principles sprang forth, giving rise to polarities and thus creating a Holy Union in a never-ending cycle. King Alpha and Queen Omega are the providers of fleshly vessels in which the Great Divine Spirit becomes a living soul.

To be blessed with Life is to be blessed with the power of Melanin, which is responsible for our human consciousness and traits (the five senses, the left side of your brain, the power to make personal decisions) and even the intuitive part, the right brain. The Pineal Gland, located in the middle of the brain, is the actual master gland. The Pineal Gland secretes Melanin and regulates all bodily functions and glands (cycles, circulation rhythms) in the body.

Having subdued this under one's comprehension, one ought to understand the fact that the first two were without fault or blemish. They were the perfect replicas of their true selves. They are the two governing principles of this world of polarities in their purest form. There was no mistaking their divine role. They are the Great Alpha and Omega, the forever interdependent couple that was already perfectly balanced and infinitely stabilised by the Great Divine All in All, the Mighty I AM THAT I AM. A World without end!

After both the physical manifestation of King Alpha and the womb manifestation of Queen Omega were fashioned [Gen. 1:27 KJV], The Great Divine blessed them and said unto them, *"Be fruitful, multiply, and replenish the earth, subdue it, and have dominion over the fish of the sea and over the fowl of the air, and the cattle, and over every living thing that moveth upon the earth."* [Gen 1:28 KJV]

Do you understand that an actual human is the embodiment of the earth, literally; all living things here, the fish, birds, cattle, and all other creatures and species, were fashioned from the stardust itself. To have dominion over the earth is to have dominion over the body. The world is a fruitful entity, and it is only right that we, in the same exactitude, be productive as it is. This is The Divine Job.

This is why Adam called his wife Eve, because she was the mother of all living things [Gen 3:20 KJV]. Therefore, in comparison, it would surely indicate that she called her husband Adam, the father of all living things. After all, they knew they were the physical envoys and manifestations of the original spiritual fore-parents of all living things, because they were aware of the power of 'Self'. They are the Alpha and the Omega, both thoroughly blessed with the power of Melanin inside-out. Both are now able to create and sustain Life in the conquest of achieving superhumanism. Initially, they are Adam (Atom) and Eve (Evolution).

To subdue the earth is to subdue the flesh under the will of our original form. That is the Holy form of the order of the Holy Trinity. A person is to achieve the highest level of humanism. This is the 'African-Centred' thought from the beginning of time. We are, individually, a culmination of this Holy Order. We are Heaven and Earth combined, with the Great Divine at the centre, even right within our heads. The right side of the brain is heaven, the left side is Earth, and our Pineal Gland, at the centre, is the Great Divine Pillar of stability.

Now, if Genesis chapter 1:28 KJV shows us that our original divine purpose is to be fruitful, multiply, and replenish the earth, then why are so many still often confused? Do keep in mind that this divine blessing was given before the 'so-called eating of the forbidden fruit' which "supposedly" brought man to his downfall.

However, in Genesis 3:16-19 (KJV), the original divine purpose of the male and the female is presented as a curse upon them, whereas at first glance it appears to be a divine blessing. It was originally ordained in the realm of spirituality, before the physical beginning of all things. This sort of blatant contradiction only leads to the contortion of the truth and the confusion of the masses.

In Genesis chapter 1:27-28 KJV, it is shown that both male and female were equally created, dependent on one another, and given their divine purpose to procreate, as the Great Supreme blessed them to be fruitful, multiply, and replenish the earth. But now, in Genesis 3:16 KJV, it is shown that to the woman sorrow shall be, and her conception shall be greatly multiplied, and her husband shall rule over her, as her desire shall be unto him.

This is the cultivation of autonomy within their union, which makes it imbalanced. Still, it is also a clear tool William Lynch uses to reverse the natural order through the 'breaking process.' It is also apparent that that version of the Bible was of value in the making of a slave as well. "As our boat sailed south on the James River, named after our Illustrious King, whose version of the Bible we cherish." - William Lynch at the beginning of his address in 1712

In Genesis 1:29 KJV, they were given all herb-bearing seeds and every tree, in which is the fruit of a tree-yielding seed, as for them it shall be for meat. But now in Genesis 3:17-18 KJV, the ground was cursed, and they had to eat of it all the days of their lives. Thorns and thistles shall it bring, and thou shall eat the herb of the land. Oh, really!

What is the purpose of one being given all herb-bearing seeds? Not for planting? The art of planting was shown before their so-called 'downfall', but now in Genesis 3:19 KJV, Adam was cursed to plant, and by the sweat of his brow shall they eat bread until they return unto the dust of the earth.

The Mystery Behind Life, Death and Resurrection

Such is the nature of just a few major contradictions that are present within the first three chapters, and it is often said that 'God is not an author of confusion', yet the confusion is plain to see. It's either that God is a liar, forbid, or simply that men are trying to conceal and suppress the truth. Yeah, must be the latter, because it was King James and his scholars who translated and compiled scriptures written thousands of years apart into one book and then called it the Holy Bible.

Adam and Eve, King Alpha and Queen Omega, the Father and Mother of all living things, had fully understood their sole divine purpose. The Great Divine had specifically designed it to be this way. These principles make physics possible, as they are the fundamental objectives in nature itself. They both knew they were equally needed and depended upon each other—neither having autonomy over the other, but each having equal rule and influence over the other. No final decision could be made unless both were in total agreement. They both understood their divine role thoroughly and the mystery called Birth/Life. The holy order of union for procreation between man and woman was imprinted in their spiritual DNA. They were the ones who awoke unto a flawless existence to be forever All-Knowing and everlasting. They are us as much as we are them. We lost our identities when they were stolen.

5
A Philosophy of 'The Divine Job'

To further whet the mind about the divine job, one needs to understand the science and art of planting. The physical evidence of all things started initially with the planting of a seed. After Adam and Eve were granted the divine blessing to procreate, they were also given the key to the science and art of the sacred task of planting. They were given all herb-bearing seeds upon the face of all the earth to be planted. They inherited such gifts from every tree, the fruit of the tree that yields seeds. [Gen 1:29 KJV]

This is the balance which nature provides to the holy governing principles of Polarity. This is the same process as with the sun and the moon, creating perfect sustainability and thus ushering great fertility and vitality through the seasons/cycles for all different types of life forms. This is the planting process, or the spiritual form of procreation, that sustains the fertility and multiplication of all earthly life.

The process of planting involves both the man and the woman, because it would be just as masturbatory as I mentioned earlier. There would be no growth without the contact or joining of two at the point of deep penetration. In this case, the man would represent the planter, whilst the woman would take on the appearance of the land. No seed grows without being planted and cared for.

The man, being the farmer or physical planter of seeds, is equipped with the necessary tools for earthly penetration. Upon penetrating the soil, he plants his seeds. No hole is dug unless it is filled with the planting of his seeds. As the seeds are buried, they are concealed within the womb of the earth. One in one, the planting process and the process of procreation are one and altogether the same.

Before planting, the land is prepared (cleansed of weeds, tilled if necessary, and fertilised with manure, etc.), ensuring perfect conditions. This shows that the woman has to fully prepare herself before being conceived with a child, and it also ensures that the father consistently meets all the necessary conditional requirements. The planting of seeds is an esoteric task of mystical divinities; likewise, sex is sacred.

Thus far, these are the physical aspects of the art of sex or of planting. The art of sex or planting is to understand how it is done physically simply, the role of the penis and the vagina and or the role of the planter and the earth.

To plant is to become knowledgeable, to gain wisdom, and to grow in understanding. To plant is to be observant and dedicated, to cultivate the virtues of patience and persistence, to recognise the importance, to grow in confidence, to gain faith, to become caring, to be filled with generosity and compassion, and to be filled with an ardour for balance. It is the acceptance of great responsibilities and becoming a protector and provider.

To plant is to develop and nurture happiness; it diminishes doubt, fosters understanding of the sacrifice of good for better, and helps overcome the grip of all fears. To plant is to hold the mystery of all truths. To plant is to bridge the spiritual realm with the physical. To plant is to understand the mysteries of Life, Death and Resurrection. To plant is to understand the principle of Charity, the possession of Universal Love, which is the key to achieving the highest level of humanism.

The divine act between the man and the woman is the fertility of their holy union, but its fulfilment is achieved through the understanding of the science of planting. This consists of the connection between the seed and the soil. Just as the seed bursts and uses a main root to connect to the earth, so the sperm bursts and connects to the mother through the means of an umbilical cord. The science of planting/sex consists of the spiritual upbringing, and this is the understanding of the actual 'purpose' of The Divine Job.

The upbringing of a child requires the continuous effort of both parents until the child reaches the age of accountability. It is the same as with planting; both the planter and the earth must be consistently dedicated to the growing, nurturing, moulding, etc., of the plant until it reaches an age at which it can stand firm on its own.

The actual science behind the art of planting/procreation is to recognise that the mother is the first teacher. In the soil, the earth teaches the seed to shed itself, grow roots, feed naturally, and then shoot upward from the ground. The exact process occurs in the uterus, though it varies slightly from woman to woman. Whatever she eats is broken down and fed to the growing foetus that has already taken root within her soil. As for the spiritual aspects, whatever she feeds her subconscious is what will be imprinted upon the child.

It is of grave importance that parents eat well before, during, and after childbirth, especially for the mother, who should remain mindful of what is fed to the child. It is a dedicated thing, just as it is with planting. Having sex under a different order, e.g., under the influence of alcohol, drugs, imbalanced thoughts, and a too-negative mindset, affects the outcome of a child conceived in such a state. A one-night stand in which either party isn't ready to be a parent will have a significant impact on a child conceived, as the mother will pass on to the fetus the entirety of what she feels. In later years, this has a significant contribution to the child's emotional or behavioural patterns.

Constant sex throughout pregnancy leaves an imprint on the child, not only because of the physical traits involved but also because of the mental implications associated with it. Sex changes the milk of a mother's breasts if another partner is introduced, whether the male or female partner is involved in promiscuity. This is very dangerous for the child because it presents another genetic transfer other than that of its original parents. Moreover, the strength of breast milk is still reduced with constant sex during pregnancy and after childbirth, even if it's only with the biological father. The negative implications are many.

Women need to understand that they are the creators of this realm. You have all the power because all power comes from you. It is you who holds the key to Life, for your womb is the gateway; you are the embodiment of the Ankh. Your importance has been somewhat hidden throughout history because you have the power to change this entire creation. It begins with self-knowledge, for you will then give birth to a new race of divine human beings who shall reconstruct and rule alongside you once stability is restored.

It is you who has the power to programme a child into what you want them to be. You are the initial software programme that downloads and imprints itself on the child's development from the earliest stages. The child is obedient unto you, acting according to what you have registered within them. As a result of your eating and drinking habits, sexual traits, and overall mindset before, during, and after conception, the beginning of this is set, and this is what induces the behavioural pattern of the entire world. Stop making your children, and then allow them to be strangers unto you. Your children's identity is the result of what you have created. You can bear a gift or a curse; either way, it is unto yourself.

Know thyself, and you shall know your child, for they are an imprint of the manifestation of your thinking. Therefore, if you do not know your child's nature, it means you do not know yourself. This is the root cause of all the troubles in the world, because people who are not aware of their true nature are used as mere pawns. They have no profound purpose, so they have become like pieces on a chessboard; they can't make a move without the hand

The Mystery Behind Life, Death and Resurrection

of another. Such a way of life is left open to exploitation, misuse and abuse, oppression and destruction, and total annihilation.

The science and art of planting lie in fully understanding both the spiritual and physical aspects of the procreation process. Through this thorough understanding, the balance of all things is maintained. It is the Universal Law in which one truly honours their original Mother and Father, not only by being fruitful but by creating divine vessels for Divine Life.

It takes far more than physical needs to raise a child; it requires substantial spiritual nurturing and protection to ensure the process is complete. As a seed is planted, it connects to the earth and to the spiritual vibrations of the planter through dedication, sacrifice, and love for the act of planting.

Regarding the child's spiritual growth, both the mother and the father must know their origins. Before the first sixteen weeks of pregnancy, or the fourth month after conception, a mother ought to be informing her subconscious about her truthful beginnings and those of the Holy Trinity, so that such information would be downloaded into the baby. After that time, the growing child begins to hear sounds from the outside world, including the voices of its parents. It is there that both father and mother can teach the child the truth by word of mouth, thoroughly imprinting divine knowledge upon the baby.

Incorporating such principles before and after conception, such as eating and drinking correctly, preparing your vessels physically, and conditioning your minds spiritually by learning the origin of all truths, would make The Divine Job complete. The honouring of your parents began within the womb; therefore, what is taught would be adapted and eventually be manifested at birth.

The world is out of balance because parents have become unbalanced, not truly self-aware. It begins with the woman suppressed, and then the man becomes the head, creating an imbalance in nature. Because balance means both are equal, this creates a single, unbroken cycle. It is the reverse principle in nature, initiated during slavery by William Lynch and other experts.

Rather than being interdependent and balanced by nature, males and females now compete for control and attempt to survive independently of one another. It is self-destructive. It is suicidal. This is what is now being imprinted upon children at birth, with mass family breakdown as children grow up fatherless and motherless. There are increases in unwanted pregnancies and abortions, especially amongst the highly pigmented communities.

Many have lost themselves, forgetting their origins and spinning like tops. Not understanding the Great Divine and the Holy Trinity is not knowing where you came from. Not knowing where you came from is not honouring your true Mother and Father and the Giver of Life. You do not understand your divine purpose, and you risk being lost forever.

After a seed is planted, there is anticipation for its growth. When it finally bursts, it brings a sigh of relief and a sense of joy. However, one recognises that this is only the beginning, as many more sacrifices lie ahead. The signs of strong, healthy crop growth indicate that your continual commitment is paying off. But it all boils down to the fruitfulness of your crops, which will be a testament to all you have done. There is no greater joy than the fruitfulness of your crops, as this is the best way a plant can honour its planter.

We represent those same crops, as we were once planted as seeds by our original foreparents. To honour our parents is to grow up in the right way, the way they genuinely want us to be. To honour our original foreparents, the incredible King Alpha and Queen Omega, is to grow spiritually by learning about their state of perfect balance, thereby conforming to such a Holy Order.

As a result, the fruitfulness of our offspring shall be holy unto the Most High, and the children of our loins shall be the most incredible honour unto the Holy Trinity. In achieving such high levels of super-humanism, the prophetic blessing to multiply and replenish the earth is truly bequeathed by the Great Divine and naturally inherited by such a disciple. Not only shall your fruits be of great sustenance, but they shall also increase and be restored rapidly, perpetuating your lineage. Not only shall your days be long upon the land, but your legacy shall continue throughout eternity, for you will soon realise that you can never truly die.

6
Of Spiritual and Physical Connection

To understand the physical realm of existence in its entirety, one must fully understand the spiritual realms and be able to connect the dots. All things began in the spiritual realm. Keeping this in mind, one ought to see the direct connection and perfect relationship between that which is physical.

- The Holy Trinity originally began as The Great Divine Nothingness (infinite Melanin), keeping its original form but replicating itself into two other energy sources. Positive and Negative. The process by which light and dark could now exist visibly was the beginning of Life spiritually.
- The Earth is the physical form of The Holy Trinity; it consists of a core or centred sun amid Positive energy, along with the content of Negative energy or is well saturated by water, but is filled with the power of Melanin, in which all physical Life began.

- The first marriage occurred amongst the Cosmos, and this is the Holy Union between the first two governing principles in which the order of polarity existed to create a perpetual Life cycle.
- In the physical realm, these were the physical forms of the Sun and the Moon: Adam and Eve, the male and the female becoming one, but also that of the earth, because it is the same two principles that are combined. The world is unisexual. The actual marriage physically is the procreation process in which the unbreakable cycle is that of a child who is genetically a combination of both the mother and father through the inheritance of 23 chromosomes from each.
- The Alpha and the Omega were the twins of creation; both required the other for continued existence. They were created simultaneously.
- Adam and Eve were fashioned and given Life at the same time. They are the twin principles of the physical world. They are like the earth, each with a balanced amount of energy, yet perfectly balanced for each other.
- Just as the Heavenly Parents gave birth to the earth through the spiritual procreation of a Melanin explosion, which was concealed in water until it was divided and became a living soul, so it is with childbirth.
- There is a Melanin explosion that takes place within the womb amongst the sperm and egg upon penetration. As a child forms, it grows within a body of water, and until the water bag bursts, the child remains in the womb, is born, takes its first breath, and becomes a living, breathtaking soul.

- The first Male and Female principle is dark matter (Melanin) because from the Divine Darkness all things came, all things are a replication of Melanin at different contents, in which it is still overall a pure spiritual light.
- The sun is a large, dark Melanin molecule, and the moon/water is filled with great Melanin. The sun does not shine, nor does the moon. The Melanin rays from the sun are absorbed by the moon and water molecules, manifesting as light and heat. Melanin appears black or brown because it absorbs all other colours except black. Therefore, the first two, Adam and Eve, were filled with Melanin inside out.
- Just as the cycle of all physical existence began with the first principle of physics, for positive energy to exist, there is a high demand for negative energy. Therefore, for the male figure to exist, there is a high demand for the female; hence, the twin birth of the Positive and Negative energies and the physical Adam and Eve.
- Just as the cycle of Life began, Eve gave birth to twins, a male and a female, Cain and Luluwa. Then unto a second set of twins; Abel and Aklia, as written in 'The Lost Books Of The Bible And The Forgotten Books Of Eden.' Seth was born to Adam and Eve after Abel died, thereby restoring the balance.
- Just as the rays from the sun are given off in abundance, so too is it with a man at the point of ejaculation. Just as the great capacity and watery element of the heavenly womb, so too is it with the physical womb. Only at the point of conception are the rays from the sun made significant. This

The Mystery Behind Life, Death and Resurrection

is the same with humans, because a man's sperm is what makes the womb become filled with a child.

- Spiritual procreation is a result of the Holy Trinity, which gives birth to the conditions necessary for Life's sustenance. Physical procreation is amongst the flesh, in which it can procreate vessels of flesh for continued bodily existence.
- Just as the sun provides rays for growth, the man offers seeds for growth. Just as the moon brings cycles or seasons in conjunction with the sun, so too does the woman, through her menstrual cycles, provide Life's sustenance (eggs/ovaries) and breast milk for the Child's growth. She is just as the night, and just as the rain is the earth's milk for substantial overnight growth, so too are the properties of breast milk.
- Just as the original two, the incredible King Alpha and Queen Omega, were blessed by the Great Divine Darkness with the power of Melanin to be fruitful, multiply, and replenish the earth, so too are people gifted with the holy powers of Melanin inside out.
- The original first two human beings were blessed with Melanin, which is the content of all Life, as it is Life itself. They made it possible for all of humanity. Melanin is a naturally civilising chemical, as its content is Life. Therefore, it is evident that the first two were naturally civilised human beings.
- In the same manner that the first two governing principles were not only given the power to procreate and sustain Life but also rule over the physical realm, the same as with the

physical founders of the human race. The man and the woman have equal rule over the provinces of the earth.

- Just as the Principles of Polarity are perfectly stable as a result of the Holy Trinity as a whole, the same is true of the earth. A human being, being the perfect representation of the planet, is also an envoy of the Holy Trinity.
  - Our mind alone is a representation of the Holy Trinity. The Right Brain represents the spiritual heaven; the Left Brain, the physical Earth; and the Master Gland, or Pineal Gland, is the Great Stabiliser that secretes Melanin and is responsible for the entire mind, giving all human characteristics and the manifestation of Life. Overall, the mind stabilises the body, which contains both forms of energy.
  - There are both male and female characteristics in each sex. In both males and females, testosterone and progesterone, the male and female hormones, are present at varying levels. It is evident that the body contains a high proportion of water and also operates with heat, which is the rays of the sun. Nothing alive under the face of the sun and the moon can survive without such principles. Polarities govern us, and each cannot coexist without the presence of the other.
- The sun, space, and the Universe are reflections of the microcosm within us and all things on a cellular level. In other words, the same processes that take place in the heavens are the same processes that occur within us in our own little world, or miniature-sized universe.
- A shift in nature, caused by imbalance, results in cataclysmic events such as earthquakes, tsunamis, volcanic

eruptions, cold fronts, extreme blizzards, excessive rainfall, severe droughts, an accelerated greenhouse effect, and global warming. The governing elements are made equal and given equal rule because autonomy engenders war, confusion, and widespread destruction.

- There is the same in both males and females. When these two become one whole, there will always be an environment of love and peace, for there is equity. A shift or rift in our nature will produce the same results as in nature itself. There is an imbalance between the opposite genders, with no love, no peace, no equity, only fighting for autonomy, family breakdowns, arguments, single-parent families, wrong spiritual downloads within children from within the womb, hate, a lack of forgiveness, confusion, domestic violence, casualties, death and destruction.
- The first law in nature is the honouring of your Heavenly parents and the Holy One who gives Life. This is the honouring of the Holy Trinity. The Earth honours the Holy Trinity by remaining perfectly balanced, not offsetting itself, and being fruitful, thereby perpetuating the way of Divine Life and Divine intervention.
- This is the same as with us being human envoys. In the womb, we were once perfectly balanced, neither male nor female. Given the power of choice, a balanced side was selected. We honour our mother and father from within the womb, for whatever is imprinted upon the child from the mother. At times, the father is what the child tends to become, because one initially honours one's parents' requests, both spiritually at first and then physically.

- The primary purpose given unto King Alpha and Queen Omega was the divine task of creating a realm of physicality in which the Great Divine may enter through the physical form to manifest and establish that which is spiritual as that which is physical. This is the physical realm of our Milky Way Galaxy, the habitation and the fullness thereof.
- This is the same principle as with the first two human beings. They were designed to achieve the highest level of superhumanism. The divine task was to sanctify procreation, in which divine vessels would be fashioned for divine life forms to walk upon the face of the earth, learning, manifesting, and establishing all truths of the spiritual realms. A person is born to achieve the highest level of superhumanism, not to be circumcised but to exist eternally.
- Heaven is our true inheritance, our rightful birthplace. We are not humans embarking on a journey of spiritual enlightenment; we are spirits of enlightenment having a human experience.
- Just as the sun is a planter of rays and the moon is a bearer of cycles, the man is a planter of life, and the woman is a bearer of multiple offspring. In the same way, the sun and the moon hold the mystery for all life on earth, the male and female principles hold the mystery of the spiritual beginnings of Life. To be the physical factors of that which is spiritual means that within us lies the mystery of Life, Death, Resurrection, and eternal existence.
- The mind is the bridge of commonality between the spiritual world and the physical world. We see the spiritual world when we sleep or when we see from within.

- At night, there is a decrease in electricity from the male principle in nature (the sun), but there is an increase in magnetism from the female principle in nature (the moon). The male principle in nature generates magnetism, which regenerates at night, whilst the female principle in nature's electricity regenerates magnetism. All are balanced by the Universal force of Melanin, which generates electromagnetic, balanced vibrations of electricity.
- This is the same process which takes place with the male and the female principle within well Melanated People (Black People) during their sleep pattern in the book 'Melanin' written by Dr Afrika. However, the Third Eye, or Pineal Gland, generates electrical electromagnetic balanced vibrations within us.
- The cyclic sleep sequence of the Earth shows that at night, that side of the Earth is physically inactive while the other side becomes physically active. This is the same occurrence in the body; to sleep is to render the body inactive, the mind voluntarily inactive, but to make the spirit voluntarily active (conscious and unconscious dreaming). When exiting sleep, the spirit is voluntarily inactive and involuntarily active. The mind is now voluntarily active, and so too is the body, under the control of the left brain. Such is the same as with the rising of the Sun, awakening that part of the Earth that was in the sleep sequence.
- The Great Divine is the Spiritual principle of all of Life's fruitfulness, multiplication, and replenishment because the Spirit is ever consistently regenerating, replicating, reenergising, and revitalising its omnipresent, omnipotent,

and omniscient nature of perfect, illustrious, ineffable perfection.
- This is the same process with the Earth, which is Melanin-enriched and a self-healing Entity in its own right, even through herbs, bushes, foods, trees, etc. For instance, spray the grass with herbicide, killing it from the roots; leave it alone, and after some time, fresh, new, lush vegetation springs up, without planting.
- As for our human body, for every given ailment, the treatment lies initially within the Spirit, as well as in the vast array of natural foods, herbs, bushes, and forest products. What is usually called a disease is a harmonising healing crisis of the body or a cleansing reaction to the actual disease, which is certain foods themselves. [For further reading, visit: www.assatashakur.org/ Science in Science by Dr Llaila O. Afrika]
- The sun works best within an organic environment, making our planet a very suitable place where the cycle of Life has been prevalent for many generations. Organic material decomposes quickly and becomes nutritious compost, which helps the Earth function better. Flesh takes longer to decompose; hence, it is buried, as its smell is most putrid and unpleasant.
- It is the same with the human body. The sun's action within our bodies is most effective at the cellular level due to melanin. Organic foods will quickly melt away and pass through one's digestive system with ease. Just as on the earth, when flesh enters, it rots. This is a root cause of the ailments our bodies develop. We have made our bodies

into burial grounds, and, as a result, they house sicknesses, and premature death becomes the playground.

All these comparisons between the two realms are to prove to you, the seeker of all truths, that all things initially began within the realm of spirituality. The physical world is evidence of what already existed within the invisible. The evidence is with us, within us, and it is us. The Earth and all physical things are evidence of the invisible. It is the proof needed to achieve superhumanism. For there to be a link between both worlds, there must be a bridge of commonality.

The mind is the bridge between the spiritual and the physical, with the Pineal Gland as the gateway. Although the spiritual world remains distinct from the physical world, it is nevertheless similar to it. It is simply a matter of experiencing another form of existence in a timeless zone.

All this would not have been possible for this long if anarchy were the order of the day. However, praise the name of the Most High Divine, for the Holy Trinity is that of perfect harmony and Universal Order. What was in the Beginning shall also be in the End. So, and forever, shall be the world without end, because the spiritual connection is unbreakable.

7
The Mystery Called Death

> "My people are destroyed for lack of knowledge" – Hosea 4:6 KJV.

Fear is a lack of knowledge. To fear something is to have a lack of knowledge concerning that which is feared. Scepticism would always be present in the absence of knowledge. Without proper knowledge, there will always be fearfulness, room for superstition and psychopathology, both mental and physical enslavement, mind and body control, no salvation, no mental, physical and spiritual elevation, a woeful life, destruction and eternal damnation of 'Self'.

Therefore, see the utmost importance of the Ancient 'African' Proverb, "MAN KNOW THYSELF."

Everyone may gain the quantity (some form of tangible value) of knowledge, but only a few can inherit the quality and authentic aesthetics of its illustrious nature. To be ignorant at heart and stubborn in mind, knowledge is of no use to that individual at all. Such is the one who knows it all, cannot be corrected, is always in competition to be better than another, compromises with the truth, is always self-righteous, is never yet wrong, and has no sense in reasoning at all.

This is so because knowledge, all by itself, puffeth up (1st Corinthians 8:1 KJV). Only a fool knows everything, but the wise know that learning is an ongoing process, for the climb in knowledge is a perpetual journey. The foundation upon which knowledge is set is the ground of humility. Knowledge is the pillar of stability, with wisdom and understanding as the scales of balance. Knowledge, Wisdom and Understanding are unto the likeness of the Holy Trinity. Together, they are the key to existence.

To the humble, knowledge is everything. It is the one thing carried to the grave through the transition. Knowledge only puffs itself within the consciousness of a human that is not stabilised correctly or balanced upon perfect grounds. Humility is the key through which sound yet profound knowledge is inherited through a conscientious awakening, spiritually and physically woven with divine wisdom and overstanding. Together, this aforementioned Holy Three is the answer to all mysteries and the secret key to eternal existence.

To fear death is to lack knowledge of it. If you don't know from whence you came, then how shall you know where to go? To understand the nature of death, one must realise one's nature at birth.

Tevin C. R. Dubé

The mystery of death lies within a simple seed. When a seed is planted, it must first die for the eye within to survive. This is the same for us at the point of conception in our mother's womb. We were all that peculiar seed, that chosen sperm that penetrated the egg or fertile ground. Each of us was the fastest, the strongest of all the other seeds in the rush or race for physical existence. You are a natural-born winner at your first race; therefore, know yourself and know your worth.

As a farmer plants his seeds, he places more than one seed in each hole dug, because some seeds are not guaranteed to germinate. This is the same upon the penetration of the vagina during the procreation process; it is the same upon the emission of the rays of the sun.

Once the right seed is planted and takes root, it sheds its outer husk. The seed is no more, but the eye lives and is transformed into a new thing, a seedling or young tree. As one was planted as a sperm within the womb of the mother, when the sperm becomes attached to the egg, it is no more. The sperm also takes root through the umbilical cord, sheds its contents, and becomes a growing fetus, then a newborn.

There is a Melanin explosion that takes place at the point of conception, just as with the 'Big Bang', because it is the point at which all creation began. This is the microcosmic replication of the entire Universe occurring within us at the molecular level.

In other words, at birth, one must first die to be reborn or transformed into something new, something much greater. The good must be sacrificed before inheriting the better. A seed is a good thing, but how much better is a plant bearing many fruits and

The Mystery Behind Life, Death and Resurrection

producing more seeds? A sperm is a good thing, but how much greater is a human being with infinite possibilities?

So, to live, one must first die, and to die means to live again. One must first begin at death to end at life, and to end at life is to start at death. To us who are alive from within the womb, death was already conquered by the Great Divine. The Great Divine, already in us, was conquered upon conception in our mother's womb. The Third Eye is what lives even when we die, just as the eye survives within a seed when it dies.

Often, I pondered death; it has been on my mind a great deal since my youth. I would bury dead insects in little matchboxes and dig them up again in three days to try to understand their processes. I was scared of death, yet still fascinated, as I had attended a great many funerals when I was a young boy. In the same way that burials took place, so too did I conduct my burials of the little creatures that died.

Growing up with such an inquisitive nature, I became deeply intrigued by the Pharaohs of ancient Kemet, the black land, or Ancient Egypt, as I flipped through the pages of the past and searched my mind. Why were the Pharaohs so captivated by death and their burials? This is a question I've asked myself many times over the years, before I began to grasp the knowledge. I sought to understand what they knew and what made them fearless in the face of death, even as they looked forward to it.

Rather than being wholly occupied with fine threads, horses and chariots, beautiful women, wealth, and gourmet foods, as soon as they were inaugurated as Pharaohs, the construction of their tombs became their primary focus and central agenda item. This gave rise to numerous significant structures that remain, such as the Great Pyramids of Giza, built by Khufu. There are several others, some of which were left abandoned, such as those of Akhenaten and his son, the 'Black Boy King', Tutankhamen (King Tut). It occurred to me that those men looked forward to death with a firm assurance of something great, and I wanted to know what it was and why. After all, it had something to do with the knowledge they acquired and were passed down, but now it is a mystery to many of us, their true descendants.

As I began to scratch the surface, it was an adamant fact that at some point in time, what was once alive must meet death; we all must die. From this point, I could easily understand the pharaoh's preparations for death. All the riches and joys of the world don't mean anything if your soul lacks the content of Life. This knowledge may be sufficient for the average mind, but as for me, I had to dig deeper by creating clefts within the surfaces of shallow truths.

At conception, the sperm dies and makes way for the fetus to develop, taking on new features and characteristics. It is evident at birth that we are no longer that tiny sperm, barely visible to the naked eye, but have been transformed into something new and improved—a living, breathing, eating, walking, talking, effectively functioning being. It's simply amazing! With all of this and so many more details, we are unique, each special and unique, each so rare, carrying its own design, each similar yet different in all aspects from the other, each invaluable and priceless.

As the fetus begins to form after the sperm dies, it is unlike anything that has ever been seen. At nine weeks, the fetus is neither male nor female, with no discernible sex differences. The fetus has human characteristics, but it is not yet like the mother or the father. The child is like the wind; it is what it is, having no form of gender, just as The Most Divine in its purest form.

At this stage, the child is in its purest form, at the point where all things began—all-knowing, all-powerful. It is like the movie 'A Curious Case of Benjamin Button', but taking place in the child's spiritual form. This is the point at which the Great Divine replicated, reconstructed and adjusted the balance of existence, just as in the beginning.

The fetus is balanced, with 23 chromosomes from the mother and 23 from the father, for a total of 46 chromosomes, which all humans share. There are rare cases in which a child may inherit an extra chromosome, causing Down syndrome and autism, but this occurs during cell division and is never inherited from either parent.

Call me crazy, but as long as I can remember, I've always told many that I genuinely believed we all had a conversation with the Most High Supreme before we were born. I said that, somehow, I knew this, but I cannot fully explain it because of the stages we undergo after birth.

My seemingly crazy belief seems to be somewhat more profound through the acquisition of Knowledge, which is divinely sustained by the soundness of Wisdom and Understanding. It is at that stage in our mother's womb, from whence we were given the power of choice. Hence, the Biblical statement which God made unto Jeremiah in the book of Jeremiah 1:5 KJV, "Before I formed thee in the belly, I knew thee: and before thou camest forth out of the womb I sanctified thee, and I ordained thee a prophet unto the nations."

At that stage, we were given the power of the Great Holy Trinity, which means we must honour it. We were instructed to honour our mother and father from within the womb and to acknowledge the Great One responsible for all existence. Hence, King David said in Psalm 139:14-15 KJV, "I will praise Thee, for I am fearfully and wonderfully made: Marvellous are thy works; and that my soul knoweth right well. My substance was not hidden from thee, when I was made in secret, and curiously wrought in the lowest parts of the earth (the womb)."

The power of choice gained its point of origin in the womb after the fetus took on the appearance of a particular gender. This process begins between 11 and 13 weeks of pregnancy. By the twentieth week, the external genitalia changes are complete, but as early as 16-18 weeks of pregnancy, the sex can be identified using ultrasound technology.

In the absence of the SRY gene (Testis-determining factor) on the Y chromosome (sex-determining region Y), a female embryo will develop. Therefore, the fetus, once neither male nor female, has now taken on the likeness of the womb-manifestation XX chromosome, or the woman. In the presence of the SRY gene or the Y chromosome, the genderless fetus has now taken on the likeness of the manifestation of the XY chromosome, or the male.

To fear death is to lack knowledge concerning death. Death is not merely about being dead but is the state of transitioning from something good into something greater. It is a shift from goodness to a paradigm of greatness.

The Mystery Behind Life, Death and Resurrection

At the start of every new cycle, there is a death. At conception, the sperm dies and becomes a foetus. When a baby is born, the fetus is no more. The beginning of a child signals the death of the baby stage. To reach the stage of a teenager, one must first die as a child. The adolescent stage is no longer present once one enters adulthood, and the end of the adult stage is when one reaches the senior citizen stage. Each is a transitional stage; thus, Life is a cycle in which Death completes it. They are both the Beginning and the Ending.

Understanding your origins as a human being is one of the most significant accomplishments of your current existence. It makes your journey even more meaningful because your 'True Purpose' would have been discovered. The road you are travelling will be carefully observed along the way, as you will become increasingly knowledgeable and further enlightened about every single point towards your next destination.

The womb is the Divine Darkness of space, from which one is formed. It is like the darkness within the earth that a planted seed needs to grow. Therefore, heaven is our birthright, our initial birthplace, but the world is now made our footstool. To be born through the vagina is to have once travelled through the Universe, and it is also the means of entrance into the realm of physicality from the realm of spirituality. Heaven is where we belong.

To enter this realm, you need the womb, or womb-manifestation, or a woman, but to leave, you need to master the knowledge of 'Self'. You need to stimulate and keep your Master Gland (Pineal Gland) active through proper eating, drinking, and knowledge-seeking. It is the only doorway through which we can return to our real homes.

This was the order in which the Pharaohs understood and looked toward the next phase in the journey of existence: through the transitional gate (Pineal Gateway), or the stage of Death, as it is called today. They knew that becoming attached to this flesh, and the things of the flesh (lusts and desires), is to be trapped within this very peculiar part of Creation, where illusions can be somewhat insurmountable. Physical things are usually regarded as greater than spiritual things. The last is placed first and is regarded as greater than the originator.

Our knowledge and understanding of our birth, of where we came from, would only be made more profound at the current stage we're at. We are no longer sperm, for that part of us has died and is no more. But look at how the transition from that stage has now truly become glorious, giving rise to the incredible vastness of the physical existence called humanity. How much greater shall the next phase be beyond the death of the flesh?

Many would celebrate their birthdays yet still fear death. How contradictory we can be in deceiving ourselves. Many look forward to their birthday, sometimes counting down the days in great anticipation. To anticipate your birthday is to anticipate your earthly departure. Every year you celebrate is a year closer to your transition.

The Pharaohs believed that one was born to attain the highest level of superhumanity. Having comprehended all that was said, one ought now to fully understand why the Pharaohs designed such elaborate tombs to be laid in upon their departure. They did not do it only out of their sheer influence upon others, but based upon the significant impact and greatness of the knowledge of the Most High. They knew the importance of the flesh in all ways, even the benefits of the once-living vessel. They ensured that they did what was necessary while alive and continued to contribute even after their deaths.

The tombs were not just packed with great riches, favourite foods, pets, and loved ones, but also with walls carved with incredible knowledge that was inherited on their journey. All things began in the realm of spirituality, and if the realm of physicality has so many things that have become well-loved and worth seeking after by humanity, how much greater shall it be in the next? Seeing such physical evidence of truth about the unforeseen in 'The Now' only entails that the transition through death from this stage to another can only signify that there is even something greater beyond this current form of our existence.

Everyone wishes to remain forever young, but the fact is that the flesh grows old daily. To reach old age is a preference, but to stay in a decrepit state is highly unlikely to be anyone's wish. Therefore, death is significant because the state of being old is to wish for something better than remaining a prisoner due to decreased mobility and an increase in the body's deterioration.

The Pharaohs were looking forward to seeing what the next transformation had in store. It makes no sense to fear death, especially when it must be faced; it is better to become knowledgeable, so that the fear of confrontation becomes a joy of acceptance. Everything in the next ought to be greater; they were confident of this because the evidence is all around them in the status they have achieved under the grace of The Most Holy One.

Growing older is often regarded favourably by many for the wrong reasons, which is why it is celebrated or greatly anticipated. This indicates a lack of knowledge, as rushing time or tasks can lead to missed vital opportunities. Many do not realise that they celebrate their death through their birthdays, but they do so wrongly because of a lack of knowledge, and rightly unto their human consciousness. The body was designed to transport us from our real home and back again. This occurs during the transition stage. The Pineal Gland is the place from which we can enter, and it is through the Pineal Gland that we shall take our exit.

Death is the planting of a seed that sheds itself, only to be reborn as a tree, perpetuating its cycle through its fertility and the reincarnation of more seeds. Death unto the flesh is to return unto seed form, as you were in the beginning, only to be replanted once more and reborn into something greater than before. It may sound absurd, but even though the face of death might not be appealing to the eyes of the living who are attached to the flesh, it is still a glorious thing. The flesh can be truly convincing, but it is designed to be short-lived. With proper knowledge of it, one would wholly realise that only great things come from it.

8
The Mystery Called Resurrection

The thought of death is a great fear that many have yet still to overcome mentally. The nature of it is truly horrendous unto the carnal mind. The sight of seeing another lying motionless within a wooden box is one of the greatest fears, if not the greatest fear, for anyone who is of the flesh. Everybody wants to go to heaven, but no one wants to die.

It is hard for many to perceive the thought that one day to come, the body which you love so much will one day be no more. Death is greatly feared by many because many were taught that no one truly knows what is thereafter. 'A dead man tells no tales, so we have no tangible evidence to show, but little do many know that we have the most experience in this field.

Apart from death at conception within the womb of our mothers, we are living signs of death and resurrection, each time someone sleeps and is then awakened. To rest is the inactivity of the body, and to sleep is the inactivity of the conscious mind. To be asleep is to become, in a conscious sense, dead to all that is physically around. There is no physical sense of touch, taste, sound, sight, or smell. To awake from this state is to be resurrected once more to the state of being conscious.

The death of the flesh is deep sleep, which is very much a form of deep meditation. One can choose to die and could die whenever one chooses, because all your energy has to be focused on the acceptance of it. This is the reason why Yeshua was able to give up the ghost in [Mathew 27:50/Luke 23:46 KJV]. It is the same as when someone wants to sleep; the mind thinks only of sleep, and the Third Eye or Pineal Gland secretes Melanin, which can be transformed into all things (as it produces Melatonin, which is responsible for sleep). Death is not the ending; it is the beginning of a new existence, as much as Life is the beginning unto death, yet still the start of something new altogether. It is the same with sleep within the physical; to sleep is to lay down the death of tiredness, and to awake is to resurrect unto the newness of strength.

I am here to explain beyond the gates of death. I have come to shatter the existing fear of death in the minds of the living. When a person dies, they have conquered the fear of death because they are no longer bound by it. This, in itself, is beneficial. However, no one wants to die because no one knows its true beauty. That's why many live in fear, even though they are aware that one day they will die. This in itself is an unstable position, because many who cower to the truth are filled with lies and are constantly oppressed. Nevertheless, to conquer death while you're still physically existing is the greatest thing, because your current existence would not be lived and restricted by fear—actual knowledge bringeth all overstanding. A seed fears not the dark but strives through it because it is a great light.

The mystery of resurrection rests within a simple seed, as I have mentioned time and again thus far. By now, one ought to understand that farming is the most divine job ever given unto man. It was given since the dawning of physical existence. Apart from being blessed to be fruitful, multiply, and replenish the earth through procreation, the first two were gifted with all herb-bearing seeds to be planted [Gen 1:28-29 KJV]. The art of planting works together with the physical form of procreation, but the spiritual upbringing of both is the science of the same process.

A farmer is to be the bringer of abundant life, a nurturer and sustainer of it as well. It is the divine order to feed and satisfy the physical needs demanded for continued physical existence. I have come to be a true farmer of the spiritual consciousness of a man who has been starving for far too long.

The procreation process is the physical re-creation of the flesh through the birth of a baby. Still, it is also the process by which the Great Divine Spirit manifests or reincarnates itself through the vessels, bringing them to life. God is already here, just waiting for us to become enlightened unto the truth of ourselves. However, the child's consciousness is separate yet unique, given to all.

Remember that what is good in the physical is even better in the spiritual. When people are constantly in search of truth physically, it only signals that the spirit is hungry and thirsty for more satisfaction, and that one's very existence depends on it. Once the appetite for knowledge opens up, it becomes insatiable. It is a switch that, once activated, cannot be easily deactivated. It's like a river flowing downhill from a mountain top. The process may be dammed, controlled and channelled through canals and turbines, but it could never be permanently stopped. You could never reverse the process of a waterfall.

Many fill their stomachs, but the spirit has been on a lifelong fast, eating greedily whatever comes before their altars. It is no wonder the world is in a mess, and so many are prematurely dying without knowledge of the truth about themselves.

One way to tell that a person takes good care of what they have is the way they take care of something that does not belong to them when given temporary possession of it.

This vessel that we are in current possession of does not belong to us, nor is the breath or Life within us titled to our ownership. Let me explain. Upon death or the state of transition, the body gives off its last breath, and this returns to the naturalness of the cosmic energy. It belongs unto the Great Divine Spirit, and that is where it returns to. The body somewhat belongs unto the Earth, and there is where it returns to, as the Earth is the possession of the Great Alpha and Omega, their child of all humanity and creatures alike.

Understanding this would make it seem as though our existence was for nothing. If the body does not belong to us, nor does the spirit, then what is the possession of my physical existence? It would almost seem that we are an amusement, that our joys and sorrows, our failures and successes, our guilt and forgiveness, our creation, and all that we endure are nothing more than a joke and an experiment.

The Mystery Behind Life, Death and Resurrection

Yes, on the other hand, one may now understand a little more of the Universal Order called Love. We were given everlasting qualities, blessed by the Great Divine, that could never truly die. We were given a body of perfect balance, sanctified by the Holy Spirit of the Great Divine (Melanin), to begin our journey toward the highest level of superhumanism. All this was initially given out of Love, so that we could save our own human consciousness by the Power of Choice. We are all given an equal opportunity to choose permanent existence.

It's like this: we were given the 'Power of Choice' to choose. To fully awaken our subconscious awareness by seeking knowledge of balance is to exist forever, just as the Holy Trinity does, because our human consciousness is what we strive to preserve. If not, it's like this: your decisions would be your fall from out of existence, and this is of little concern unto the Great Divine, even the Holy Trinity. The world is without end, and the Great Divine is everlasting. It is human consciousness that is at issue. It is a simple choice to save or condemn our own existence.

The Philosophy of Resurrection after Death:

Let us take an okra seed, for example. Any sensible farmer would know that the average seed takes at least three days to burst, just as a sperm does upon the egg's penetration. The question is, how can something die and yet still live? It is logical to think that if something is alive, it's alive, and if something is dead, it is dead. It's either one or the other; it cannot be both at the same time. We all know that when death strikes, whatever it takes up has come to a permanent end. At least this is what we were taught, because it is true for the flesh.

Nevertheless, this is not the case with a seed. When the seed is planted, after three days it is dead and no more, but the eye doth live. How is it even possible? It is the same as with procreation. As the seed is planted by the man, in time it would become a child, but at the expense of the parents dying, because they are giving part of their lives to their offspring, while at the same time becoming alive through their fertility.

When something dies, that is the end of it, and this much is still true, up to a point. If Life is bounded by Death and Death is bounded by Life, then which is higher than the other? Neither of them, for they are both interdependent, each existing because of the other. There must be something Higher, something Greater, the order of polarities does not mandate that, but is in fact the initiator of that order, the very head of all perpetuating cycles, and yet still operating independently from all.

Once the okra seed is planted and the eye bursts, the seed is no longer viable and is long gone. But from it a new thing rises, an okra tree. The seed, once suitable for planting, had died, yet still lives again through the resurrection of a tree of perpetuation.

Life is the only thing that has walked through Death and returned alive; as much as what was once dead returns through the gates of Life, alive. Death is a threshold still connected to life; it is a doorway to new awakening and new possibilities, even a doorway to perpetuating everlastingness. This is so because the Great Divine Spirit is the only Being to have ever existed within both Life and Death—simply because the Most High existed before all things and is all things. Therefore, Existence is higher than both Life and Death and is responsible for their presence.

The Mystery Behind Life, Death and Resurrection

When a person dies, they have entered a state of transition, being recreated into something new. The term to die or to be dead is such an overrated and exaggerated statement that has continually renewed the fear in the minds of many across past generations and even at this very moment.

Take, for instance, the case of an 'African' or anyone with high levels of Melanin. When dead, the body emits more electromagnetism. This is why 'Africans', most of the time, tend to appear darker after death. If someone dies, everything about them must stop permanently! This shows that Melanin is responsible for Life, as even after Death, Melanin allows the body to emit energy, meaning it is still, in some way, alive. Melanin supports the perpetuation of Life, even through Death. This is how the 'so-called dead' communicate with us now, no longer by physical traits of the senses but through connections of electromagnetism, higher frequencies, and even (instinctive) emotions.

One may now understand that death is truly a celebration, because the consciousness of that person can now be reached through a deeper emotional connection, not through sadness but through Love and fond memories.

Before we came into physical existence, we were initially buried as a seed in the grounds of our mother's womb. We first died as sperm but were reborn and resurrected as a foetus, then as a child, and now we are what we are right now. It's like the metamorphosis of a butterfly. It starts as an egg, then becomes a larva (caterpillar), then a pupa (cocoon), and finally a butterfly, after which the cycle begins again.

We commenced this Life as a seed, and what was in the beginning shall be in the end. Therefore, a seed we began as, and a seed we shall end as, but only to start anew and afresh. To know where you came from will automatically teach you where you are destined to be.

When the body is taken to the grave, people often call it a burial, but it is more than that: a significant planting. The body has become a ready seed to be planted, just as the sperm was at first.

Any good farmer knows that whenever one goes to plant, there must be a celebration of the heart, a connection of love and joy, never sadness or hunger, as these add to the vitality, growth, and fruitfulness of the crops. These are the spiritual aspects of the physical work, in conjunction with the spiritual. It establishes a profound spiritual link with the departed soul, who has become an ancestral presence; hence the old saying that a funeral is a time for celebration. The person is in a better place, as they have now passed on from a place of time unto eternity. A place where physical sorrows have no power; hence the lyrical line, "Death O Death O meh Lord. When my body goes down in the grave, then my soul leaps for joy."

The Great Divine is responsible for all existence, including the cycle of Life and Death. The Great Divine is neither male nor female but the principle of Life, manifested in both, giving each its own identity. The Great Divine is above gender, Life and Death, and above all things, high and low. The Most High Supreme Being has never lived nor ever died. The Great Divine knows what it is to always be in existence. One may suppress and harm the fabulous

The Mystery Behind Life, Death and Resurrection

Melanin presence that is of the flesh, but not that which is of the entire Universal Order. It is only delaying the inevitable.

When a person enters a transitional state or ceases to move, as in deep sleep, this does not signify death. The Life within, the invisible breath, is given off, and that breath returns to its original form. The body returns to the ground, becoming one with Earth, a living being, yet in its original form. The breath emitted is present in everyone alive, and they still breathe. The body laid to rest is present in everybody alive, and they still eat as it goes back into all living things, herbs, trees, fruits, animals, and us. Hence, understand that the true Holy Communion is an earthly thing, not merely that of communion on Sunday. This is the accurate representation of what the Messiah was talking about: the partaking of natural drinks, herbs, and vegetation.

If grass is sprayed with poison and killed from its roots, it dies and withers completely, but after a time, it regrows, making the once-dead vegetation lush again. This proves that the Earth is a Living Being. Even though the body breathes involuntarily, when someone transitions and breathes no more, it doesn't mean the air isn't breathable. Many are still alive, and many are now taking their first breath of Life, or should I say their first pain of Death, as they cry. The state of transitioning is an act to free the breath that is somewhat trapped within the flesh, in that it is an involuntary action, proving its independence from the flesh in which it is housed. Death is the act in which the flesh gives up the Life it temporarily possessed.

When a seed is planted in the earth, even though it dies, it still lives, proving that the world is alive. Therefore, when the flesh passes and is grown, the body will no longer be, but shall be transformed, becoming one with the living earth and thus a part of all living things again.

With this understanding, let us take it one step further toward understanding the true purpose of our existence. Beyond realising and understanding our divine purpose, we are aware of consciousness, for we are envoys of the Holy Trinity. We are temporarily given access to the power of the Holy Trinity to become aware or to be given proof of the profound choice to be everlasting.

Our vessels are subject to the Governing Principles of King Alpha and Queen Omega, from whom both male and female principles sprang. All Life is the result of the all-powerful Melanin, which belongs to the Great Divine Spirit, the Infinitely Divine Darkness, as we see it with human eyes. This refers to the presence of fish in a pond dug and left to accumulate over time. It mysteriously teems with aquatic life. Now, what is your true purpose for one's existence, knowing that all you currently have does not belong to thee? No, it is not so; what belongs to us is our human consciousness.

Our true purpose for being here is to follow our divine order of procreation and to awaken our inner consciousness by utilising the Power of the Trinity that was invested within us. In doing so, the seed of knowledge would be planted in the soil of humility and watered and nurtured by wisdom and understanding. We are here to achieve the highest possible human level, and this is achieved through the power of choice to preserve and restore the purity of our human consciousness.

The Mystery Behind Life, Death and Resurrection

The only time a human is truly dead is the moment when they have not yet awakened their consciousness. To be unaware of the origin of all things, even of oneself, would only ensure that you have ceased fighting for your existence, giving up your natural birthright. Remember, our breath is a gift from the Most High; our body is a gift from the stardust of our true Parents, who are already eternally perpetuated. But our human consciousness needs the pillar of knowledge, along with the balances of wisdom and understanding of our beginning, to know profoundly about our end, which only ensures that we make our existence permanently perpetual as well.

Just as a seed is planted, the eye doth live; it is the same with the body that is grown; the Third Eye lives. There is an old saying: elders prophesied that, after someone dies, their consciousness or essence becomes aware within three days that they have left the physical world.

Just as the eye bursts in the seed and resurrects, the same principle applies to us after death. Remember, Yeshua said in John 2:19 KJV, "Destroy this temple and in three days I shall raise it."

This three-day period is the same time in which the eye of a seed takes root and is resurrected into the newness of Life. This same three-day period, even at the time of death and burial, marks the start of the body's decomposition process, but it is your human consciousness that shall resurrect from out of the ground unto the Most High that dwells within the flesh. This is why Yeshua taught the knowledge of truth for three years: it gave rise to the resurrection of the dead man Lazarus and to the dead maiden human consciousness—the enlightenment of divine knowledge through teachings from the foundations of both spiritual and physical existence.

This is the proper form of resurrection. No spirit remains in the grave, for it returns to the Great Divine from the moment you transition. The body returns to the earth once more, but your human consciousness is what resurrects from the grave and goes to the judiciary of the Holy Trinity to be judged. All human consciousness shall resurrect, but those who take truthful knowledge to their grave shall be transformed into the newness of an ever-perpetuating existence, just as an okra tree is fruitful, multiplying and replenishing itself by producing many more seeds.

The human body is a tree yielding fruit. The fruit, which is yet still of the body, bears seeds. The seed, which is the fruit that is yet still of the body, becomes the ready seed that will soon be good for replanting. The human body remains the seed, but the eye within is the human consciousness that emerged through the Pineal Doorway.

The true resurrection is not merely the learning of truth but the lifestyle acceptance of it, which increases your overall vibrations through Melanin overstanding. To conquer such physically is to be absorbed spiritually, which gives complete awareness unto the human consciousness, enabling us to overcome all things. We not only achieve superhumanism but also permanently possess it. We are, after all, highly spirited, constantly growing and evolving naturally.

We already have death as our inheritance. In our everyday existence, we are constantly in transition. It is axiomatic that we shed and regenerate dead skin cells at the microscopic level every day. Being here in the physical is the spirit learning to master death to attain perfection, not only in Life but also to exist eternally in supreme bliss.

Just as millions of sperm or semen (sea-of-men) are released into the uterus, we were all, and still are, being released into the earth through continuous childbirth.

The earth appears like a ball or, more precisely, like an egg within a woman's ovary. And we, as a whole, are the newness of sperm within the earth, searching for that next perfect point of deep penetration. We are struggling to reach that new point of conception, to be further transformed into something brand new. It is just like another nine-month process for the nine ether beings.

We are literally going through the same procreation process within the womb. But we have forgotten that journey within the womb as a result of the trauma experienced during the process of birth. We are now going through a similar process, but this familiar territory has become unfamiliar.

Similarly, just as the microcosmic process of procreation unfolds, so too are we, who are within the earth, still within the womb of the entire Universe. Not everyone will achieve that new transformation because of the deep sleep many choose to remain in. Many continue to go through the trials of Birth and Decay, failing to use every experience to catapult themselves into a higher form of existence. They become trapped by judgment, hatred, envy and jealousy, hypocrisy, rancour and calumny. There is good to be found in all things for the enlightened, but for the sleeping, it is only when in their carnal favour.

The inverse effect in this life is that if we stand opposite each other, my right becomes your left, and your left becomes my right. There is a greater good to be found in all things. Who has eyes to see, let them see, and who has ears to hear, let them hear. Nevertheless, many have chosen to become antigens within the earth (womb). In response, antibodies are naturally produced to combat the problem (it can take the form of natural disasters, life-changing events, and revolutions), among other examples.

Every single sperm has the opportunity to penetrate, but only those chosen by the egg can enter. It is the same with us; hence the statement, "Many are called, but the chosen are few." As a result, the world witnessed the remarkable transformations of great individuals such as Marcus Garvey, Nelson Mandela, Malcolm X, Martin Luther King, Bob Marley, and many more. They shall witness this new uprising.

The resurrection of the flesh is through continuous childbirth. Even though each individual has a different identity, the commonality we all share, and will continue to share, is that of the Spirit/Superior Force, even the Dominant Gene.

However, the actual resurrection, while being part of the flesh, is to realise that you are actually what you are not. It is to be fully aware and awakened to the fact that you have been nothing more than the Spirit you have been searching for. Your daily walk with Death is to reopen your Third Eye unto a more abundantly everlasting form of existence.

Accepting this profound truth would then allow you to achieve the ultimate form of resurrection. You would then be connected with the ascended masters and sages of the past as you begin to attain the highest possible levels of superhumanism. You would then start to see and become what you are not, apart from what you already consider yourself to be (a mere mortal being).

At this stage, you would already have become an infusion and one with All Things on a spiritual level. It is then to be converted into absolutely 'Nothing' to become entirely centred with the very source of super-consciousness by becoming super-conscious yourself. Just as your sperm transported that super-conscious awareness, you are now transporting and learning to further develop yourselves from it. The sperm has just been transformed into a body in which you can now summon new thoughts and ideas from the unknown, in other words, from The Great Beyond. You were already All-Knowing, but now you are born Knowing-All.

9
The Mystery Behind the Brain

The mind has only one main sense, and this is not the pituitary gland in the middle of the brain that secretes growth hormones, which have erroneously been called the master gland. The main sense in which the body has a sense is the Pineal Gland, the actual master gland and the centre of the brain.

The Pineal Gland secretes Melanin, which regulates all bodily functions and glands. The brain is Melanin-dependent and uses Melanin in many forms. Melanin is the vital chemical that makes life itself possible in all forms. It is present in all things, both animate and inanimate. The Pineal Gland's secretion of Melanin is what makes and keeps the body functioning. Melanin is what grants the right brain its intuitive nature and allows the left brain to make the five physical senses dominant. The Pineal Gland is the Third Eye from which the abundance of all things flows.

To understand the very beginning of 'The Beginning' itself, one must first understand the network of Melanin. Melanin is not usually taught about, yet it appears often in biology, not under the name Melanin, but as the Nuclei, the dark or essential part of a cell or nucleus. To completely understand yourself, you need to understand your nature, especially the Melanated content; the study of the Pineal Gland.

Melanin is responsible for the civilisation of all humanity. The more Melanin, the more civilised a race becomes. Dr Afrika, in his book 'Melanin', and many others have laid down profound evidence through their extensive but painstaking studies over the years to help illuminate the minds of many. Melanated people need to be more mindful of what types of foods, drinks, synthetic drugs, illegal substances, etc., they intake, because it leads to becoming anti-Melanin. To anti-Melanate yourself is to become self-destructive; it is akin to committing suicide. Nature cannot go against itself; the results are always catastrophic, creating anarchy—Black-on-Black crimes, drive-bys, etc.

'The Teachings Of Ptahhotep, The Oldest Book In The World', edited by Asa G. Hillard III, Larry Williams and Nia Damali, shows significant evidence of civilisation in ancient times. Hieroglyphics was the name the Greeks used for the ancient writings, Mdw Ntr [sometimes called Mdw (word) Netcher (God)], the word of the Gods, or simply Holy Writings, thousands of years after this writing system was created. It existed long before there were even ancient Greeks. Mdw Ntr is modern-day 'Africa' and the world's oldest recorded writing system. This writing system appears fully developed, indicating it must have existed long before ancient Kemet (Egypt) or Ta-Seti came into being. This pre-Kemetic civilisation was native to Alkebulan, a heavily hued, well-pigmented civilisation. They were the first nation-states. This fact supports the development of early civilisation in the ancient Hapi (Nile) Valley.

From this point, it takes little effort to identify the link between Kemetic texts and Biblical literature, 'Greek Philosophy', and Eastern religions. Kemetic texts, from the earliest writing system, are the antecedents of all other writings. No wonder many 'African' sister nations went to Ancient Kemet for advanced learning. It is evident throughout the Bible, as Abraham journeyed to Egypt (Gen 12:14 KJV), and Joseph the dreamer was sold to the Ishmaelites, only to become the first command after the Pharaoh of Egypt (Gen 39:1 KJV), even unto the time Yeshua was taken to Egypt (Matthew 2:13 KJV).

This and more are evidence that humanity has always been civilised, from ancient times to the beginnings of modern civilisation. However, it only attests that, before those first nation-states were founded, humane civilisation was already in place. It is now a proven fact that melanin is an excellent civilising chemical that consistently reproduces itself and has existed since the beginning. It is said that the oldest University on Earth is located in Africa. It is the University of Al-Kamouine [founded in 859 AD, Fez, Morocco]. European universities, such as Oxford, came almost three hundred years after the 'Africans'. The First People studied the Universe [Astronomy], hence the word University (The Universe City).

Nevertheless, in 2015, a Caucasian college professor considered himself fortunate to be working in three distinct areas of biology: immunology, genetics, and reproduction. On the genetic side, he deduced that there are Neanderthal genes in the human genome, and the proportion is quite significant, at 5-7%, based on comparisons of human genes. They used genetic methods to determine how long Neanderthals and humans were a single species and where the common ancestor was. Neanderthals originated in the Neander Valley, and modern humans originated in Africa. He further stated that people of European and Asian ancestry share about 7%- 10% of their genes with Neanderthals. However, Africans who left Africa show no evidence of Neanderthal genes or admixture. So, they are the real pure humans, Homo sapiens.

The Pineal Gland is responsible for making a human being human; therefore, the more Melanin one has, the more human one is. As stated by Dr Afrika, 'Blacks are people who are well Melanated inside-out and are more human than any other race upon the face of the earth. Melanin is the content of all Life; it is the content of pure humanity. To become anti-Melanin or to suppress its secretion is to become less of a human being.'

Tevin C. R. Dubé

10
The Mystery Behind Dreams

To understand the nature of one's dreams is to understand the nature in which the mind works. The way in which the mind operates is by means of the Pineal Gland or Master Gland. The Pineal Gland is responsible for the production/secretion of Melanin, both actively and inactively, voluntary and involuntary actions of the entire bodily unit as a whole.

Sleep is the inactivity of the conscious mind. Rest is the inactivity of the body. To be asleep is to shut down the left side of the brain, which is responsible for all physical traits of the body.

During sleep, neuroscientist Patricia L. Brooks and John H. Pever found that in the brain, the neurotransmitters gamma-aminobutyric acid (GABA) and glycine cause rapid eye movement (REM) sleep paralysis. REM is a result of the Pineal Gland Vibrations.

To dream is to envision or to see Life in a timeless state. They say that up to 70% of your dream is the truth as to what is physically taking place around you in your daily life.

To dream is an emotional bodily movement, a psychic dream trance. This is the mystical works of the Third Eye or Pineal Gland. Melanin is the indestructible force of the Great Divine Spirit. Through the Pineal Gland and the secretion of Melanin, we can strongly connect with the Most High. We can hear sounds with the ear and sounds that the physical ear cannot. It is through our intuitive right brain that we can listen to the inner voices of reason, compassion, and the Most Holy and Great Divine One. It is that which makes us spirited by nature, and nothing, nor anyone, could truly stop it. Melanin is the harmony in all things.

Prayer is an essential aspect of an individual's life. Praying is self-communication, which is why studies have shown that people who often talk to themselves are least likely to go insane. To pray is to communicate with oneself, being alone and contemplating or conversing in one's mind. It is to be in deep thought, questioning all things, and searching for divine inspiration in the carrying out of one's task.

To pray is to stimulate the Pineal Gland, to awaken your intuitive part of the brain, which is voluntarily inactive whilst the left brain and body are voluntarily active. To kneel in silent prayer is not only a representation of reverence but also a tell-tale sign to others that you need some time to be alone with your own thoughts.

Praying is about exercising your intuition while being physically awake, and it helps you become aware during REM sleep or a dream trance. To use only the left brain is to communicate through physical means, whereas to utilise the right brain effectively is to communicate through spiritual means. The brain as a whole is a bridge between the spiritual and the physical, with the sole point of connection being the Pineal Gland.

As I always tell many, if you are not dreaming at all, then something is definitely wrong with your consciousness. I would then ask how often you pray. I would recommend praying more often, but mainly the goal is to spend more time alone, channelling your own thoughts and communicating with your subconscious. No telephone, TV or other electronic devices. Maybe fifteen-minute aerobic sessions or reading material to help open up the brain's dimensions.

To dream is to be given a tour by the Great Divine Spirit within, into the spiritual realms. It prepares you to become familiar with the operations of the timeless zone. At times, dreams may seem long yet remain within the physical, lasting only a few minutes. Exercising your right brain/subconscious mind while you're awake is excellent because it increases your awareness of many great things. It stimulates the pineal gland, allowing it to function for you and bridging the gap between the spiritual and the physical.

The Pineal Gland is associated with heightened spirituality and greater information storage because Melanin is the central core unit of the entire Universe. Therefore, the Pineal Gland is the central core unit of the mind; it is the access point to the vast memory storage of the Universe within the mind. This is what makes the brain (apart from its enormous storage capacity) the most excellent physical computer network ever known to human consciousness. All truthful inspiration that was manifested into all physical forms came out of a single thought of ingenuity. All things are based on the functions and operations of Melanin.

Often, when one dreams, it becomes apparent to one's physical consciousness only after awakening from sleep that one was dreaming. Why, most of the time, are we not even aware of it in that moment? This shows how little control we have over the gifts we were given, because we know so little about ourselves.

"Do not disturb a great man or distract his attention when he is occupied, trying to understand his task. When he is thus occupied, he strips his body through the love of what he does. Love for the work which they do brings men closer to God. These are the people who succeed in what they do." – Ptahhotep

Being physically active while still exercising your intuitive mind by awakening its usual inactivity during physical inactivity is one of the most remarkable things. By doing so, you awaken your true human subconscious, which personifies us as proper conscious awareness. As a result, when one enters the psychic dream trance, our subconscious, under much greater exercise, would only make us consciously aware within our dreams.

The more one becomes conscious of the self in the timeless state, the greater the spiritual growth. It means that you are finally connecting to your true nature, and more so to the Most High, as you stimulate the Pineal Gland, absorb strength from the significant Melanin secretion, and tap into the Great Reservoir of the powers of the Holy Trinity.

This is the acceleration in spiritual growth, in which many great truths are learnt, thus leading to the upward climb of human consciousness, or 'Jacob's Ladder', towards the achievement of the highest level of superhumanism. The spirit is always ahead of the flesh; the human consciousness, in time, the body/the physical mind would be up to par with the spiritual knowledge. Hence, understand the profound awareness Daniel attained upon entering the dream/real world, gaining visions and understanding of the end [Daniel 7, 10, & 12, KJV].

Sleep paralysis, or the feeling of being held down in one's sleep, is a phenomenon in which a person, either during falling asleep (hypnagogia) or upon waking (hypnopompia), temporarily experiences an inability to move, speak, or react. It is a 'transitional state' between wakefulness and sleep, characterised by muscle atonia (muscle weakness).

This much is physically true, but what about the spiritual aspects associated with it? To sleep is to enter a state in which both the physical mind and body become inactive, while the right brain automatically becomes fully responsive or active. To dream is to be in the transitional state between wakefulness and sleep. To sleep is to be on the fine line that separates life from transition.

Entering the state of sleep paralysis can be a very terrifying experience. This is because, where knowledge is lacking, the conditions are ideal for the growth of fear. You are rendered physically unresponsive, yet subconsciously awakened. In this state, your physical traits have no power save that of your current consciousness.

Sleep paralysis lies between the states of life and death, yet it also serves as a sign that there is a conscious state beyond the transitional stage of death. In this sleep state, one becomes physically comatose yet remains conscious as a human being, thanks to the Great Divine Spirit.

Being held down in your sleep, causing sleep paralysis, is the result of the Pineal Gland through the REM zone. This is the Great Divine Spirit itself, testing the strength of one's human consciousness or 'will power.' It is a test of worth to see how deserving you are of its Divine Nature; hence the reason why the Most High called the chosen human Israel, meaning the one who wrestles with God in Hebrew.

The Pineal Gland secretes Melanin (the content of Life), which the brain depends on and uses in many ways. The Pineal Gland works in association with the right brain to provide the inactive human consciousness with evidence of a spiritual world that exists in an alternate dimension during sleep.

Truthful knowledge is the overcoming of all fears, as fear only sprouts because of a lack of knowing. When one has entered the REM state of sleep paralysis, be joyful and do not be afraid; it is not evil, nor are the works of demons; it is simply a visit by the Most Divine Creator. It is such an honour to be appointed for a direct visit by the Most Divine One.

To be in the state of sleep paralysis is to reach the greatest state of self-communication ever. Prayer is the only constructive thing, because when the wits of your physical actions are cut off, your consciousness is ever abundant, which proves that it is the most significant attribute and strength of being human. The 'will' of the consciousness of the mind is the strongest quality we have in our possession. This is a thought-oriented realm. Therefore, learn and train yourself to harness the Power of Mind.

In this state, one need not fear the Most High, for that is never the intention of the Great Divine—we were created to understand all that was placed before us and given to us. One is born to achieve the highest level of superhumanism, and to do so is to understand the Most Divine in its purest form.

No man could truly teach you about 'God' except by the nature of 'God' itself. To awaken your intuition constantly is to question the Spirit of the Most High. Inspiration, as a result, is the answer given. The intuitive inner consciousness/voice is also the source of the responses given, whether in the form of guidance, correction, or profound understanding. Moreover, to dream is also to be given significant reactions from the Most High Divine, but to become humanly conscious in that spiritual state as a result of practising spirituality in the physical state. It allows you to receive the truths of all things, both those connected to the spiritual and those connected to the physical.

All is a divine blessing through divine intervention. One may now be able to use their Third Eye vision effectively to discern all truths. This profoundly keen sight would immediately identify mystical divinities in all forms. Today it might manifest in physical forms such as a bird, a bee, a tree, a seed, even a stone, etc., and tomorrow by means of a profound dream, déjà vu, a vision or insight (flash) of the spiritual realm.

Fear not the Most High, for fear arises from a lack of knowledge, and because of that lack, the people of 'God' are destroyed. Sleep paralysis is not a sleeping disorder, but the point at which all existence exists. Fear not, because the Great Darkness that one's consciousness perceives is the Great Divine Spirit within, which has conquered all things, as all things were created by it. Know that it is the Great Divine, so through prayer entreat the Most High pleasantly, for in that time spiritual growth is given, profound knowledge is gained. The Power and Stability of the Holy Trinity are inherited.

Yes, one should be grateful. The power to instinctively return from the spiritual to the physical is attained, and one's consciousness is being elevated. So, fear not, nor resist the Great Divine in a frivolous attempt to fight one's own self from climbing the levels of superhumanism. Be joyful, for the forever-existing Entity, the Perpetuator of all never-ending principles, has called many but has been limited to choosing a few because of our lack of knowledge of ourselves. Be celebratory of such, for in those specific appointed times, one is being strengthened and tested for the walk of eternity. It is the spiritual preparation after the completion of the physical journey. To return unto the physical realm from the state of sleep paralysis is to be renewed in spirit and to be resurrected unto the knowledge of a profound but conscientious understanding. Remember, we are spirits having a human experience.

11
The State of Being Imbalanced

This world is perpetually driven by two major polarities, Positive Energy and Negative Energy. In whatever we do, one would somewhat realise that there is always an adverse effect. Nonetheless, if one has a keen sense of sight and overstanding, one would realise that all things in this realm of polarities give way to each other. They all work hand-in-hand.

To gain strength, one must rest, and to properly rest, one must actively lose strength. The night gives way for the day, and the day makes way for the night. As a result of light, there is a shadow, and if a shadow is present, it proves that there is light. All these and more are simple signs that, together, there is a state of perfect balance.

The story of humanity's origins has been dramatically altered since the dawn of 'Modern Civilisation'. The oldest surviving book, the teachings of Ptahhotep (18-page papyrus and wooden tablet), is evidence of the first nation-state of Ta-Seti and the subsequent establishment of Ancient Kemet (Egypt), showing that the earliest people came from the Nile Valley.

The reason I say this and genuinely believe it is true is simply because of the historical finds by both past and present philanthropists. The discovery of the 'Zinjanthropus' or "East African man" remains found by Richard Leakey near the east shore of Lake Roudolf in Kenya in 1470. The skull dates back millions of years, making it primitive in the direct lineage of man. However, on March 4th, 2015, a 2.8-million-year-old jawbone was pulled out from a hilltop in Addis Ababa, Ethiopia.

As I've stated earlier, the first two human beings were the embodiment of the Holy Trinity itself. The first man and the first woman were in their purest form; they were not born of the flesh and came into the world all-knowing and all-powerful. They came to start the Life Cycle; therefore, they fully understood their purpose. Their job was to create divine vessels for divine life and to teach the human consciousness that was to come into existence within the flesh to become a permanent existence.

These fossils are merely evidence that human life has existed for millions of years. Who knows how long civilised humanity has existed? Time is an illusion because no one can honestly date how long the Earth has actually existed; furthermore, there is no historical evidence or remains of the first individuals.

However, I do believe that Adam and Eve were the first two, and that they existed long before the Biblical book of Genesis, written by Moses. The Biblical literature referring to the first two was tied to a story that existed aeons before.

The state of imbalance arose from the 'power of choice' given unto human consciousness. To become imbalanced is to break the natural order of things that were initially set in the foundation of physical existence. Take, for instance, nature. Without the presence of humankind, the seasons would still take place because the principles of flesh do not govern nature, but work through it. Nature is always harmonious, as each season gives way to the other. They are constantly agreeable. Spring gives way to summer; summer gives way to autumn; autumn gives way to winter; and winter gives way to spring.

The first point of imbalance arose with the advent of mankind, as they were the first to commit such an act. It is shown in the Bible with the so-called 'Adam and Eve' at the appointed time. Genesis 6 KJV shows how the first imbalance in nature began amongst that family, "and thy desire shall be to thy husband, and he shall rule over thee." Autonomy entered the relationship, and now, instead of being governed by each other equally as nature demands, there is self-rule—one being on top, reducing the other to the bottom.

The moon is pointless without the sun, and the sun is meaningless without the moon. If there were no sun, there would be only night, and all life on Earth would become extinct. If there were no moon, one half of the Earth would be in permanent daylight and the other in permanent night, and all life would become extinct. The Earth would not rotate without the moon's gravitational presence. If the woman is suppressed, then divine life would become extinct, because she is psychologically stripped of her natural inheritance and forced into a 'slave-like' relationship in which nothing good is imprinted upon her offspring. The implication is similar for the man as well.

From whence the 'blame game' began, the man blames the woman, and the woman blames the man, but neither blames themselves. The effectiveness of this life lies in the man and the woman coming together as one, thus becoming the very foundation of Love upon which a true family is built. Nature designed it so that both are interdependent. The sun, or positive energy, was given rule over the day, whilst the moon, or negative energy, was given rule over the night; together, they rule over the entire earth. Both know their respective roles, and neither seeks autonomy.

Perpetuating imbalance disrupts family togetherness, bringing evil upon them. Evil began with humanity; it started with the power of choice given to our human consciousness. Evil is the consistent perpetuation of an act that creates an imbalance. The persistence of this imbalance over time renders the flesh animalistic. To be of an animal nature is not to operate by sensible judgment but to act on animal-like instinct. A tame tiger's animal instinct will make it attack and eat its owner when hungry if not fed on time. It is the nature of the beast to attack and eat flesh when it's hungry, as nature provides.

As written in Genesis 1:28 KJV, after God blessed Adam and Eve and gave them their divine gift of procreation, verse 29 states that God gave them a sacred task. They were given herb-bearing seeds, and the seeds are to be planted solely. They were also instructed that the fruits from the herbs were to be used as 'meat' (as a meal, not flesh). Verse 30 states, "I have given every herb for meat, and it was so."

Tevin C. R. Dubé

Food plays a significant role in the imbalance of modernised civilisation. Again, it is we who have the power to choose whether to be balanced or perpetuate our imbalance by constantly choosing not to become stable in our daily lives. In the very beginning, we were required to be true vegetarians, a vegan lifestyle.

'You are what you eat'—the mantra states. Crunchy foods, green organic herbs, fruits, other herb-bearing seeds, pulses, ground nuts, yams, and similar foods are all great embodiments of longevity. A turtle is a testament to this quality.

Meat, meaning flesh, was never mentioned in the beginning of days because it hinders not only the flesh but also the mind and the spirit. What we choose to eat and drink significantly influences our health and behavioural patterns.

A keen observation by a good friend of mine was made about a cat and its prey. He said, "The cat likes to eat the head of the animal because it adapts the instincts of that animal, making it easy to catch another every time. Think about it. Why do you think a cat plays with its catch after it masters its art of catching the specific prey? It is simply learning all its other escape techniques, in which the cat becomes a master hunter when pursuing that prey. After learning enough through playing, it then eats the head." – Keion Atiba Collymore.

To eat is to become, literally, what you've taken in. To constantly eat foods that are only high in fat is to become overweight, gain high cholesterol in the arteries, and cause clogged veins. To drink excessive alcohol is to overheat one's system, become highly intoxicated, and damage body and brain cells. One adapts the instinct of what they are eating, whether it is blood or vegetables. You pass more gas after eating red beans because they are a gassy food, etc., and the list goes on.

People have become significantly imbalanced due to consuming animal foods that were never meant for human digestion. Consistently eating flesh like flesh-eating animals makes one just like them. Your life expectancy is shortened just as theirs; meat rapidly ages the body as it rots within it, especially in domesticated animals. However, organic foods (free of chemical content) and proper drinks (mostly fresh water) replenish and regenerate the body. The sun is more effective within an organic environment; the same applies to us. Our bodies are more effective when replenished organically.

I genuinely believe that in the true Biblical days of the origins of man, the order of being good/balanced was followed. It is evident in the Biblical records of the oldest men who lived. Adam lived 930 years [Gen 5:5 KJV], Seth lived 912 years [Gen 5:8 KJV], Enos lived 905 years [Gen 5:11 KJV], Kenan lived 910 years [Gen 5:14 KJV], Mahalalel lived 895 years [Gen 5:17 KJV], Jared lived 962 years [Gen 5:20 KJV], Lamech lived 777 years [Gen 5:21 KJV], Enoch lived 365 years before God took him [Gen 5:22-24 KJV], Methuselah lived 969 years [Gen 5:27 KJV], the oldest recorded man who lived, and Noah lived 950 years [Gen 9:29 KJV]. This is what was recorded. What about the vast amount of knowledge that was never written but passed down verbally or from master to apprentice?

If such were understood in the days of Moses, then one ought to understand the statutes or instruction, precepts or negatives

Moses gave concerning the eating of clean and unclean animals [Leviticus 11 KJV]; and even the forbidden eating of blood [Leviticus 17:10-14 KJV].

Dr Llaila Afrika provides substantial evidence concerning the importance of foods, drinks, and drugs (legal and illegal) in relation to Melanin, especially within the African Diaspora, since 'Blacks' are the most Melanated of any race. He shows that many are becoming anti-Melanin, which triggers a series of adverse effects. For instance, eating too many sweets when Melanin already provides a natural sugary content; the intake of too much alcohol when your body already has a high alcohol content because of Melanin, which significantly helps the body to cool down; eating foods that destabilise your chemical hormones when Melanin already provides for such; the intake of too much sodium/salt when Melanin is a natural provider of such as well.

To become anti-melanin is to become less of a human being. It reduces many to an inhumane or cannibalistic state. It diminishes the capacity for compassion and forgiveness, and for sound judgment (all causes of Black-on-Black crimes, White-on-Black crimes, Black-on-White crimes, and White-on-White crimes, etc.). It reduces the civilising content that an actual human possesses, and brings physical weakness (with diseases and sicknesses as a good warning). It also causes spiritual illness due to the suppression of the Pineal Gland. The lack of herbal treatment and the reliance on synthetic drugs give way to freakish egg development in the female offspring and freakish sperm development in the male offspring, hence giving birth to freakish children in nature.

Children are born with pigmentation disorders (albinism), autism, and Down syndrome. Poor eating and drinking habits and a lack of self-knowledge usher the body into a rapid state of senility and premature death. Overall, this is a significant imbalance that will destroy all humanity if our ways and actions continue to be perpetuated in this manner.

If Moses, being a chosen man of God, filled with all manner of truthful knowledge and sound of mind, had been given all instructions, they would be as clear as in the beginning, when his fingers wrote them in Genesis. Only herbs bearing seed shall be consumed, as it were, the ways of the ancient ancestors who were before him.

As Dr Afrika stated, to become anti-Melanin is to become subjected to sexual misuse, because Melanin is the provider and stabiliser of hormones. Hence, understand how eating and drinking have a great deal to do with our imbalanced nature, ways, and behavioural patterns. Do you see why Moses stated in Leviticus 17:14 KJV, "Ye shall eat the blood of no manner of flesh; for the life of all flesh is the blood thereof; whosoever eateth shall be cut off." You become detached from the content of Life itself, the suppression of the Pineal Gland (the secretion of Melanin). You become detached/cut off from the full connection of the Spirit of the Most High.

Engaging in oral sex and ingesting another's genetic material through the mouth is also the eating of blood. A man's sperm and a woman's vaginal secretions are both genetic material. They are the content of the blood. To become anti-melanin is to regress towards an animal nature as one becomes less human. You are what you eat, and an animal's nature is arguably the lowest degree in life. Only animals have uncommon sex, eat uncommonly, and act uncommonly because of the degree of their spirited nature and what nature has designed them to be. Melanin is the content of all things higher and superior; therefore, the Melanin within and without us is to be treated reverently and dealt with most sacredly.

The body is the temple of the Most High, the Great Divine Spirit abiding there. Within heaven is the throne set. The Pineal Gland is the throne upon which the Great Divine dwells within the mind, stabilising the scales of balance on either side.

As for the concept of Cain and Abel and their offerings, it appears to be a total contradiction in my own opinion [Genesis 4:3-5 KJV]. If in the beginning the Lord ordained Adam and Eve with the divine blessing and task of planting seeds and eating only that which is an herb or fruit bearing seeds, then it somewhat makes the Lord an author of confusion? God forbid, for yea it is not so, for man's own ways are the epitome of confusion.

The body is the temple of the Great I Am; our mind is the altar where we lay down our supplications unto the Most High, in which we would be further given instructions. What was in the beginning, so also shall it be in the end. The sacrifices that Cain and Abel made were a plot of reversed psychology.

When I was a young boy, I would offer my food first to God so that God might have the first share. One day I said, "Lord, I know You would not eat any food because You are a spirit and spirits don't get hungry. But Lord, why would You make all these nice fruits like mango and all these foods we cook and like to eat, and

The Mystery Behind Life, Death and Resurrection

You don't like to eat any of them? Well, Lord, even though You wouldn't eat, taste it and eat through me."

This was my childish thinking when my father was still alive. I was about 6-7 years old at the time. Today, I can fully comprehend how advanced my thinking was as a child, though I was high-spirited by nature. Melanin, the infinite power of the Most High, is capable of all things. Melanin is the content of all Life, and yes, through us the Great Divine lives.

No one has ever become sick from eating raw organics or from following a healthy, balanced diet that consists only of that which grows naturally from the earth's soil. This is acceptable unto the Most High, as it increases the vast productivity of Melanin within the body and stimulates the Pineal Gland, enabling it to operate efficiently. The Spirit of the Most High is well able to move freely within such a one.

This body is so unique that it would reroute its operations to accommodate new changes, such as those related to fasting. After some time, the body would adjust to the new settings and changes associated with the fast undertaken, allowing it to become routine.

Therefore, it makes perfect sense that the sacrifice most acceptable unto 'God' between Cain and Abel was not the firstlings of the flocks but the first fruit of the ground. Herbs will always rejoice over flesh. Hence, one may now clearly see the importance of the food set in the beginning [Genesis 1-29-30 KJV].

Moreover, this proper eating is more evident in the statutes and instructions given by Moses. It becomes a symbol of the strength Samson inherited, as his mother received instructions about what should and should not be eaten or drunk [Judges 13]. The evidence shows that certain foods can render a woman barren or free her from barrenness. It also shows that both parents should be mindful of what they eat before, during, and after conception, as well as during the upbringing of a child.

Daniel demonstrated his understanding from the outset, as his lifestyle was that of a true vegan. He refused to defile himself with King Nebuchadnezzar's meat and wine, choosing pulse [edible seeds from leguminous plants, peas, lentils, etc.] and water (Daniel 1:8-12 KJV).

It was said unto Zacharias and his barren wife, Elizabeth, who was also stricken in age, concerning their son John (the Baptist) [Luke 1:15 KJV]. The same applied to the birth of Yeshua, as Mary was said to have been fed with holy food (manner) from heaven. All these and more demonstrate the importance of nutrition and its association with the balance or imbalance of the world, which is of utmost importance.

All things in the beginning were perfectly balanced and reasonable. Evil arose after men made a conscientious decision, exercising their free will. To perpetuate our choices of imbalance is to bring great evil upon not just ourselves but the generation of our loins. Evil is the result of our making, and it is we who shall feel the hell of it, not 'God.' It is we who are given the chance to exist forever; hence, the proper instructions from the beginning shall attest and bear witness in the end. From whence all things began is where all things shall end, but to begin anew and afresh. The world is a cycle in which we abide. It only makes sense insofar as it is understood.

12
Man Know Thyself

In life, there are always levels, processes, and phases that animate and inanimate things must go through. It is the way of this world; it is the way this realm of physicality was initially established. 'Change is inevitable, for the only thing constant is change.

The evidence of it is as real as all the things that meet the eye every day. It is evident with us from the point of conception as a sperm, and then the formation of a fetus, unto the likeness of a child [male/female], then until birth is given unto the child. Afterwards, the process continues from infancy through the toddler years, childhood, puberty, adolescence, adulthood, middle age, and senior years/infancy state (dependent once more).

It is further evident with the stages of plants, animals, stones, mountains, the land, seas, etc., because in time or cycles, all these things change that are under the face of the sun. Even space is in constant change, as it is continuously expanding.

This is a world of physicality, and we were the first civilised and highly intellectual beings to bear witness to all that was laid before us. The power of choice was endowed from within the womb; we were given authority and rule over the physical world. This power to rule was given to us to maintain and care for our home, and caring for the environment meant we were caring for ourselves.

If perfect balance were always maintained, there would be no global epidemic such as global warming, because no one would abuse the authority given to them. To abuse your jurisdiction is not only to oppress another but also to oppress our earthly abode and, by extension, yourself as well. From this come earthquakes, triggering tsunamis and volcanic eruptions; hurricanes, tornadoes, cold fronts, mudslides, droughts, flash floods, and other extreme weather cataclysms of mass destruction.

This is the result of perpetuating one's imbalanced state, in which the perpetuating act is what we coined as evil, for it brings self-destruction and the destruction of the innocent. Hence, understand that we are the very embodiment of our own human essence (consciousness), which we feed upon regularly. We are the physical representation of that which may help, hinder or suppress us spiritually. After our state of transitioning from the realm of the physical unto the realm of spirituality, we become that in which we were from whence we walked within flesh.

There was no Lucifer who caused humanity to sin and fall from glory. It was man who brought sin upon themselves, and with it came the sudden fall from glory. It was the perpetuation of their wrongful act, in which they suppressed the flow of the Most High Supreme within, that hindered the content of Melanin. They lowered themselves to the status of mere mortals, in which they began to possess the lower laws of nature, just as animals, and brought chaos, death, and destruction.

The Law of Ma'at – God needs you to come into the world. Fulfilling God's need is the highest act of love, and only through your love for God can you fulfill your love for others. Become the Love of God in the world for the protection of the world.

Everyone knows that Satan can't physically harm a human being, but he can persuade or entice the mind into committing evil. First of all, how do you know Satan is a he? In the case of a spirit, which is energy, how can one tell whether it is male or female? This in itself is a tell-tale sign of a lifelong daze or trance that the minds of many were and still are in.

I have never seen the devil take a gun and shoot a man to death, stab someone, rape someone, rob someone, or be jealous of another man's possession. I have observed only men committing these acts. I have never seen Satan physically enslave another race or lead many to genocide. I have never seen Satan force someone to commit suicide. This is so because Satan can't physically harm us, but can tempt the mind.

Satan is a figment of our imagination, to which we gave life and whose fear ruled our thoughts for centuries. While I was undergoing a Gate-Keepers training session on uplifting men within our community at the Toco Foundation in Toco, under the late Michael Als, in 2010, I met a fascinating middle-aged man of East Indian descent. He told me, "Last night I had a bizarre dream. I dreamt the Devil dropping to his knees, praying to God, crying and saying, 'Lord, how come I am getting all the blame for all the sins that men themselves are choosing to commit'."

Over the years, I kept this dream alive in my mind, and today it makes perfect sense. Satan is a figment of the mind, and many today use it as a scapegoat to blame their own actions and continuous imbalances. And now, when the benefits of our daily actions are being reaped, one wants to blame the Devil rather than themselves.

A mistake is easily forgivable because every human is entitled to, and has made, many mistakes daily. However, to perpetuate the error is to first make it a mental repetition by monopolising thoughts, which will initiate the repetition of words and eventually lead to repeating the act or deed.

Nothing can control an individual's thoughts unless they allow their thoughts to be manipulated. We all have a choice, and this power has somewhat become mundane. Satan was the first to perpetuate imbalance; evil was the creation of man's own doing.

Due to a continuous state of imbalance, the body becomes at war within itself. Human consciousness is now in conflict with the spiritual subconscious. This is 'The Great War of The Lord'. To suppress the contents of Life within is to make the human consciousness self-righteous in all ways, which makes the heart and mind of a human stubborn. It is we, as the human consciousness, who choose to be a devil's advocate or an angelic entity, both physical and spiritual.

As I've said, this is a Life of levels, and it's as if we have signed up for the army regiment and our applications have been accepted.

One may start as a Private [PVT, holding no rank], Private 2 [PV2], Private First Class [PFC], Specialist [SPC], Corporal [CPL], Sergeant [SGT], Staff Sergeant [SSG], Sergeant First Class [SFC], Master Sergeant [MSG], First Sergeant [1SG], Sergeant Major [SGM], Command Sergeant Major [CSM], and then Sergeant Major of the Army [SMA]. The head above all is the President.

This is the level of Angels. The Third Sphere consists of lower Angels, Archangels, and Principalities. The Second Sphere of higher Angels includes Powers, Virtues, and Dominions. The First Sphere of the highest Angels includes Thrones, Cherubim, and Seraphim, each ranked from the least to the highest within each sphere, with separate tasks. However, the head of all these is the Almighty Divine.

These are the ranks of Demons, from highest to lowest: Satan, representing Pride; Beelzebub, representing Envy; Sathanus, representing Wrath; Abaddon, representing Sloth; Mammon, representing Greed, Avarice and Covetousness; Belphegor, representing Gluttony; and Asmodeus, representing Lust.

Tevin C. R. Dubé

13
God, Satan, Angels and Demons

We were born to achieve the highest level of superhumanism. To achieve these levels of humanism, one must go through phases to achieve one's desired rank. To achieve one's rank, one must be dedicated towards the tests painstakingly in their journey, and strong-willed in the completion of their tasks. To be climbing constantly, one needs to remain focused, never losing sight of one's true purpose through persistence and perseverance. The same ladder on which someone can achieve a higher rank is the same ladder on which they could be demoted.

The Most High Divine has always been here; for the Earth and the fullness thereof, is that of the great All in All. The Divine Supreme is the Melanin Content in which the Earth itself is the way that it is. It is the essence of all living things and is responsible for all that exists.

The Mystery Behind Life, Death and Resurrection

"In my Father's house, there are many mansions," this much is true, for the Universe is the original house, and within it are the mansions of many galaxies. We are in the Milky Way Mansion/Galaxy. We are already within heaven, for even though we are on Earth, Earth is still within the Milky Way Galaxy, and the Milky Way Galaxy and all within it are part of the entire Universe, including Heaven. What special heaven are we looking for? What God from above are we awaiting? The Most High Supreme is already here, reigning not just universally but within the heart and flesh of the conscious.

Attaining the highest levels of superhumanism is to become the physical embodiment of angels. Hence, the Biblical saying in Hebrews 13:2 KJV, "Be not forgetful to entertain strangers: for thereby some have entertained angels unawares." To fail to attain the highest levels of superhumanism is to become the physical embodiment of the seven deadly acts of imbalance or to be demoted to the lowest ranks in humanism, or 'hell'.

To reach the highest level in our humanist quest, one must raise their vibrations or Pineal acceleration by seeking and maintaining balance. This fosters a stronger connection to the Great Divine within and helps one become attuned to Nature itself. As a result, the 'great phenomenon' occurs, a profound shift in one's spiritual nature as the knowledge of all truths is released. This is the sage mode of human consciousness. The more one ascends through spiritual enhancement, the greater one's angelic rank becomes.

After one has increased their overall vibration to the highest order in the angelic order, there is only one stage left—the state of becoming 'Godlike' or one with 'God', the 'God-Man' upon the face of the Earth. This is the highest attainable level in humanism, because one reaches the Infinite Level, becoming one with the Most Divine Creator at the highest level of all things. This is the order of fervent Charity, or the order of Love Absolute.

To decrease one's vibration is to lower oneself to the lowest rank in the quest for superhumanism. One ought to understand by now that depictions of Satan and demons are the result of human traits. These take the form of Pride, Envy, Wrath, Sloth (laziness/procrastination), Greed and Covetousness, Gluttony, and Lust.

Ptahhotep said, *"Greed is a grievous sickness that has no cure. There is no treatment for it. It embroils fathers, mothers, and the mother's brothers. It parts the wife from the husband. Greed is a compound of all evil things. It is a bundle of all the hateful.*

These traits have always been the world's problems, and their perpetuation is the main reason for them. To stray from the path of higher knowledge, wisdom and overstanding is to become the embodiment of all imbalances. It is first to become Anti-Melanin, Anti-Love, Anti-God, even the least Anti-Messiah/Christ.

'The upholder is worse than the thief.' To make a mistake is part of life, but to perpetuate it out of sheer will and choice, conscientiously, is to be held accountable. To confess to the Most High and atone for one's wrongs is to achieve inner peace, thus becoming stronger. But one must first be able to forgive oneself before forgiving another is truly accomplished. To not make amends with oneself is to be conflicted and at war with 'Self', hence one becomes weaker, only seeking self-righteous excuses, and is rendered impotent spiritually and destroyed physically.

The Mystery Behind Life, Death and Resurrection

Remember, it is our human consciousness we are trying to save from eternal damnation. The body belongs unto the Earth, the spirit unto the Great Divine Being, but our human consciousness is our own identity, an everlasting gift given unto us by the Holy Trinity. Resurrection is for all, but it is what one shall be resurrected unto. All seeds planted are resurrected; some are the resurrection of fruit-bearing trees, whilst others are the resurrection of an injurious weed. One rises unto glorification in the end, whilst another is constantly reproved and cut down.

Remember, our physical journey is preparation for the spiritual voyage in the next phase of continued existence. The one thing we can take with us is the intrinsic nature of actual knowledge. Whatever we adapt to our human consciousness in the physical world, we would become its true embodiment as we roam the realms of spirituality, becoming one with that nature. The frequency or energy you harbour in the physical would become part of your human entity or consciousness.

Take, for instance, two individuals in the physical realm who meet but are operating at different frequencies. One is practising the higher laws of balance, whilst the other is free-minded to whatever. Upon meeting, one seeks to impose one's ways on the other. This is a clash of frequencies: an agreeable with a disagreeable. There is no common ground. This may be interpreted as a clash between an angelic and a demonic force.

Now, say these two have transitioned and become the embodiment of what they were processing in the physical. They have become ancestors. Here are two in the physical world who have taken a similar path to the previous two. At the same frequency level as the two preceding ones, both human essences would be strummed, creating a reincarnated reenactment or retake between the present two. The only difference is that both spirited forms of human consciousness are simultaneously angels and demons.

As each is upon the opposing frequency at the same time, the ancestral link would be a helping force unto either of the two, making them both appear as an angelic force. But as the two become in contrast to each other, both essences would appear as bad vibes or a demon to the other. At the appointed time, both are not agreeable because one is compelling the other to enforce their beliefs upon the other.

Throughout this journey, I have come to understand that we are the physical evidence of the spiritual realms. The first man who perpetuated imbalances by continually breaking the Laws of Balance became the first Devil as a human. As for those who conscientiously choose these paths of imbalance, they become the physical embodiment of eternal damnation through non-existence.

What we feed our minds is what we will eventually become. Within us, the Great Divine already exists, maintaining the perfect balance of all things. To become imbalanced is to go against the Pillar of Stability. We then become at war within ourselves as we defile the temple of the Most High, for we dwell within the House of the Great Divine.

The initial fight between God and Satan, angel and demon, Christ and Anti-Christ occurs within the mind. It is the war between the human consciousness of imperfection and the Spiritual

Consciousness of all perfections. To wrestle with 'God' is the human consciousness questioning itself or the Spiritual nature within, in which one tends to awaken spiritually. To fight is to remain in a sound sleep and become truly dead, because to go against one's entire nature is to be circumcised out of existence.

It is we humans who can become the true embodiment of 'God' or Satan (the adversary of one's own thoughts), a faithful Angel or Demon; it is we who can become a Messiah or an Anti-agent. The power of choice is ours, but the author and finisher of your faith is still the Great Divine within you, writing and guiding your path along the way, even the Holy Trinity.

We are the holders of our own faith; we were given control of our destiny. This is why the Great Divine vowed to guide a man along whatever path he may choose. Guidance is always given to each individual, but it can be accepted, disregarded, or discarded.

Ptahhotep said, *"He who hears is beloved by God. He whom God hates does not hear. The heart makes of its owner a hearer and a none-hearer."*

The power of choice holds the faith towards eternal existence or eternal damnation. If the Most High Divine gives the boat, then one remains stranded on the shore, with no other point across.

Tevin C. R. Dubé

14
Time

The concept of time has been woven into the fabric of our physical existence, as history dates it back to the dawn of the so-called period when man became civilised.

For thousands of years, various devices have been used to map and record time. Our current time of measurement, the sexagesimal system, dates back to approximately 2000 BC in Sumer. The Ancient Egyptians divided the day into two 12-hour periods and used large obelisks to track the sun's movement. They also developed water clocks, which were probably first used in the Precinct of Amen-Re and later outside Egypt. The Ancient Greeks frequently employed them, calling them clepsydrae.

The only actual existence of time is that of "Now". All things, the past, present and future are taking place in "The Now". The only evidence of time is that it is occurring now.

The Ancient 'African-Centred' thought concerning time holds that "Time exists in now" and is eternal and cyclic. The future, past,

The Mystery Behind Life, Death and Resurrection

and present are combined. Time is based on the beginning and ending of an event and is composed of the seen and unseen (Spiritual, God-manifested) cause of an event—commonly called coloured people's time. The event fixes time. For example, the seasons of spring, summer, winter and autumn start according to nature's unseen clock.

Before the past could exist, it must occur "Now". The present exists because it is happening "Now". For the future to occur, it is also the happenings of "The Now." This is the fact that the actual presence of time is the time of "Now."

Yesterday is still today, and tomorrow is still today. The only difference is that we have separated them simply due to Earth's orbital motion. It is we who have created both a past and a future. All our days, weeks, months, years, decades, scores, centuries and millennia have been just one day. We are the creators of our own future, for it is we who actually create a tomorrow. It's because we are living in the now. Time is mapped by our existence in 'the now', for we are all a Moment in the Time-consistency. We are all in total control of our destinies once we truly know ourselves at this given point in our current existence in the Time Sequence of Now.

Hence, one may now understand the notion that the Biblical Prophets preached repentance, for the time is at hand. When the phrase 'Live Life as if there is no tomorrow' is used, it is simply because there truly is no tomorrow; everything is happening now, and all things are going to take place today.

Time is like a rolling ball. It is constant in itself, but to us in the physical world, it operates cyclically, and for quite some time, men have been mapping its sequences. Time has no face; it is just like the roundness of a ball. When the ball rolls, it may change course; in that moment, its trajectory has changed, and its timing has shifted accordingly.

Time is constant, yet in the face of inevitable change, it also appears to have changed. Many changes have occurred since the mapping of time, but one constant is that they all happened during the period of 'Time Consistency'.

The ball may roll in many directions, changing its position but never losing its shape. The changes in the world may have taken different directions, but time has never lost its structure. Time is consistently now, and this is what no one can stop. One may alter its course, but for a while; the inevitability of it achieving what it wants is greater than the influence or grip of a mere mortal instrument of flesh.

As a whole, humanity has created specific periods of time as markers or representations of the present. The time of the Egyptian Civilisation may be no more, but the ways of that particular period still linger. There may no longer be Pharaohs, but there are tycoons. No fine chariots with horses as the best means of transport, but now there are luxurious cars and private jets. There may no longer be great castles, but there are massive mansions and so much more. Their customs may be a bit different from the norm, but they are pretty similar in many aspects. The ball of direction may have changed, but the structure of time remains the same.

The time for change is 'now'. The power to change anything can only be realised now; to delay oneself is to lose track of the true essence of what time demands or stands for. People need to grasp the Concept of now fully.

As a result of our roundish Earth's cyclic motion, rotating under the Moon's gravitational pull, time is now measured by the brighter light of the day and the lesser light of the night. With this particular rotation, hours were counted; days became weeks, weeks months, and months years. But then, altogether, the calendar came into existence, and now, today, we are in the 21st century since its origins.

However, the remains of the oldest book in the world, written by Ptahhotep after the barbaric Alexander had ordered the destruction of the temple of Alexandria, provide evidence that civilised people had long existed before the history of the so-called modern civilisation or the first established nations of Ta-Seti and Kemet.

The Sun is fixed at the centre of our solar system, but Earth's rotation maintains the balance that allows life to thrive on it. If this were not the case, not only would all life become extinct, but there would be no such thing as time, thereby demonstrating that time is constant in nature. Time is always in the present, eternally cyclical, but it is mapped only by events or seasons.

Time is a single, continuous day that never ends. The true time behind time is that there is no actual time. The existence of a sort of time came into being as a result of the Holy Trinity. Time could only be measured in the realm of physicality. However, just as the timeless zone in the spiritual realm is timeless, the physical is also timeless; it is the flesh that is somewhat bounded by polarities and the changes associated with the passage of time. This is evident in that we have all been given a brief moment to experience and bear witness to the wonders of all existence, but it can only be lengthened by the knowledge of knowing thyself. Time is for a spirit to have a brief but maximised physical or human experience.

Our human identity is the most ingenious device created to aid our human awareness in beholding all things and acknowledging the Great One responsible for them. This realm in which we are is but a test to raise our consciousness to the highest order of knowledge, physically, so that we would be bound for an existence of eternity through a constant form of evolution.

To delay time is to become trapped in the spell or illusion of procrastination. It is through the illusion of time that many are destroyed. The body that was given unto us came with a time of expiration. The thought is destroying many who have time on their side. We are all given a moment or period in which one may temporarily alter that particular period in a timely existence. The true power for us to utilise is to make perfect use of the powers of 'The Now'.

Time is of the essence for us all in achieving our levels by raising our vibrations. We have lost purpose in our existence, and now the truth seems to be a far-fetched lie, while that far-fetched lie is seemingly the truth. The sound of the truth is strange to our ears, and the vision of it has become a blur to the eyes. Many have demanded the illusion of lies, making it their reality, in which many are mentally ill yet still unaware, trying to teach their perceived ways of sanity through their conscious insanity. Many are unconsciously insane, suffering from conscious insanity.

Classifying age as a measure of how old you are is to become psychologically impaired. The body you are given is under your authority, and it responds to commands issued through genuine thoughts and emotions. Your feelings are the one thing that truly never lies. To be old is to feel old. To set a time in which you believe you would become old is unto the fulfilment of you.

The days of the average human life being three scores and ten (70 years, as written in the prayer of Moses, Psalm 90:10 KJV) are made so for us. It is we who eat, drink and live unnaturally, and make ourselves genuinely believe and make it so, in which the body ages under our own command.

The true power of time is the power of 'Now'. By the Power of 'Now', we are given temporary possession, in which we can gain control over our destiny. With the power to control one's destiny, we can now leave a physical marker of our current existence before we return unto the actual state from whence all things originally came: The Timeless State of all Creation.

Awake and arise, harness the 'Powers of Now', cement your rightful legacy, and achieve and establish your human right to be Free truly. To truly understand the 'Power of Now' is to be in existence For-I-Ver-More. Selah.

15
The Spiritual Network

The physical networking of things is laid out so intricately that simplicity is still woven into its extraordinary yet extravagant ineffability. The unspeakable nature of so many things is what truly captivates the beholder. As awe floods through such an individual's system, inchoately, it is hard to conceptualise all that is associated with it. If this much can be said about the physical, how much greater is that of the spiritual, in which all things initially commenced?

As with a computer system, the Spiritual system's network is not comparable; it has only a few similarities. Just as the computer unit contains a motherboard, which is the system's main circuitry, the Great Divine is the system's main circuitry, and the heart/brain is the same within the human body. The power supply for the main computer is located in the Unit and is identical to the others. All other components, including the monitor, mouse, keyboard, and speakers, connect to the Unit to form a fully functional system. The same is true of the body, as all its parts come together to form a fully functioning system. As for the spiritual network, the Great Divine created branches within which the Holy Trinity became a functional system.

The primary power source that enables the entire computer system to function is electrical energy. The primary power source sustaining the human system is the energy of Life, which is the power source of Melanin (dark matter/energy). The main power supply that makes the Holy Trinity possible is the Great Divine Spirit, whose Power originates in the self-empowering supply of Universal Love.

A computer communicates by representing information in binary code. Within the body, there are diverse ways it communicates internally, but cells are the primary transmitters: there are trillions of them, each carrying out a different function. The mind is the central core unit that transmits information through the spinal cord, which then distributes energy throughout the entire system. The only difference between these two is that the computer uses artificial intelligence, whereas the human system does not.

The spiritual network, or Google, is far more complex than either of the two mentioned above, but there is one significant difference. The central unit of the body, the Pineal Gland, is the direct link to the spiritual network. The body is the computer system through which the spirit communicates or channels divine inspiration.

The Universe is always in constant communication. Space is filled with numerous high-frequency sounds that are deafening to the unaided ear, yet it appears tranquil. However, these transmissions can only be heard clearly through the mystical properties of Melanin. Melanin is the most excellent receiver and storage unit, through which we can access the entire knowledge of the Universe and communicate directly with it. Melanin is a receptor; therefore, we are the receptors. This is the property of every Melanin pigment found within the skin and the body. Know yourself and become more open to receiving, because the Universe is forever giving. A blessing is measured not by how it is presented but by how well it is received.

Given that the body/mind is, in a sense, artificial intelligence relative to the trustworthy source of all networking, the programming given unto each unit, the imprint of our unique identities or human consciousness, one ought to be mindful of the energies they choose to house within their systems.

From a human perspective, the origins of all things began with a simple thought. Through entertaining, dwelling on, or perpetuating thoughts, it becomes evident as it escapes through words. Through the repetition of words, they correspond to the mind and fuel one another, taking the form of action or becoming evident in our deeds. Therefore, an idle mind keeps an idle tongue and makes for idle ways.

"Well did you know the pen is stronger than the knife and they can kill you once but they can't kill you twice? Did you know destruction of the flesh is not the ending to life? Fear not of the anti-Christ. Did you know that I exist before the earth, and did you know my eyes are windows to the world? Did you know you can't go a Zion and a wear jheri curls, can't tell the boys from the girls? The body is just a vehicle transporting the soul; it's what's inside a

people is beauty to behold. Fear not of evil, everyday them flesh it grow old, changes of the time take the toll." – Damian Marley (lyrics from the song, 'It was written')

Your works in "The Now" would be the mark of your existence, but they would also be the evidence that would seal your faith within the eternal realm. One thing has remained consistent in The Now: the legacy that was initiated by many.

The works of many great human beings endure, bearing witness to their continued existence. Having passed on from this realm unto the other, the fruits of their labours are still the gift that keeps on giving. They have never yet died. The evidence is clear in the case of Pharaoh Akhenaten, the teachings of Ptahhotep, Apollonius of Tyana, Buddha, Noah, Abraham, Moses, Jacob, Joseph, King David, King Solomon, and even Yeshua.

The consistency of such evidence remains evident today. It is apparent in the works of the Hon. Marcus Mosiah Garvey, Emperor Haile Selassie I, Bob Marley, Peter Tosh, Dr Martin Luther King, Malcolm X, Garnett Silk, Jacob Miller, Mother Theresa, Dr Maya Angelo, and Nelson Mandela. There are still many great pioneers who are alive, carrying on great legacies and preserving the lineage of righteousness.

Those who have left such great legacies have not yet died; they continue to exist through their works. Their legacies are what continue to add to their existence as we strum upon them, and we connect with their entities, in which they are still present with us in 'The Now'. They have now become our ancestors, ready to communicate with us, having become one with the higher Spiritual Networking Connection of all things.

Tevin C. R. Dubé

"And it was written, up in the Book of Life, that the man shall, endure forevermore." – Stephen Marley (Chorus from the song – It was written)

As for those of the past who practised not the ways of balance but harboured the lower laws of an imbalanced nature, which continue to plague all existence, the same applies to them; their works are what many may dwell upon, but only for some time. The accountability of their actions is constantly held against them, which hinders them from the higher realms or heaven and sinks them further out of existence into the lowest realms of unconsciousness or hell. The true heaven is eternal and glorious, whereas the actual hell is not a lake of fire but being eternally cut off from remembrance.

For those of us who are alive, the energies we choose to harbour will reflect the type of conjuring that takes place within the realms of spirituality. Our mind is the initial ground on which one may summon past human entities or human consciousness, and/or ancestral links. It becomes evident in what is drawn towards an individual. Energy is attracted to energy in the same way emotions are attuned to one another.

Be forever mindful of these things. Fail not in the pursuit of understanding one's truthful purpose; the quest is always an ongoing process. Death is the end of this flesh but the beginning of a new process, a new stage, a new evolution and transformation. There is no end to the heights except the start of higher heights. Draw and home the energies of eternity that are already within thee, yet still roundabout all things. Become saturated by it by

Knowing Thyself, and thou shalt become eternal, even immortal in flesh, for the seeds of procreation are already chosen.

To not know or lose the true purpose of one's existence is to become chaff, easily blown in the wind without any form of direction. This shows a lack of knowing thyself, with no stable ground on which a foundation can be established. This instability causes one to harbour the lowest energies through imbalances, and one will circumcise oneself out of existence when time takes its toll. This is the true nature and embodiment of death concerning our human awareness.

Marcus Garvey said, *"Read! Read! Read! And never stop until you discover the knowledge of the Universe."*

Reading is an essential factor. Even if you read and cannot retain every single word, the subconscious mind does. It retains every single word. You need to understand the power of Melanin and why, during slavery, reading was forbidden to slaves and was severely punished. Reading and learning are essential to freeing your mind.

King David said, *"My heart is inditing a good matter, I speak of the things which I have made touching the King: my tongue is the pen of a ready writer."* – [Psalm 45:1 KJV]

"And when they bring you into the synagogues, and unto magistrates, and powers, take ye no thought how or what thing ye shall answer, or what ye shall say: For the Holy Ghost shall teach you in the same hour what ye ought to say." – Yeshua [Luke12:11-12 KJV]

All this is proof that through the stimulation of the Pineal Gland, one would be able to retain the correct set of knowledge at any given point in time. Melanin is the entire store of all knowledge beheld by the Universal mind of the Great Divine Spirit. The Power of the Great Divine is ever flowing like a stream.

Therefore, Read! Read! Read! And make your works approved by retaining as much truth as you can, so that when you return unto the Spiritual Networking, you will become a far superior embodiment of enlightenment. Every word, every detail, and every aspect will be grasped and explored infinitely. To read is not only to inherit the knowledge of the profound writer of truths but also that of all the profound entities that have visited such a person in their sheer focus, dedication, and Love for what they do. How much greater shall you be, for more shall be added unto you. So, every new generation shall be greater than those of the past.

Marcus Garvey professed that his ancestors called out to him from beyond the grave. He also said that in the great fight to free 'Africans,' look for him in the whirlwind that comes with the once enslaved ancestors.

The decision is ours at this appointed time. Melanin is an absorbent factor that never refuses to absorb what is naturally good. It is your choice whether to be a human or a divine being in whatever you choose to do or think. No knowledge is ever wasted, but you would become the embodiment of that which you perpetuate. Therefore, be the personification of a true Universal Being, and without a doubt, you would indefinitely become the Light of the World and a key element in The Spiritual Network of the Most Divine Holy Being.

16
Of Concerning 'The End'

Not being adherent to simple truths only portrays stubbornness of heart and hardening of mind. Such acts are associated with a lack of common sense. To lack common sense is to lack the foundation on which all sources of knowledge begin. To lack knowledge is to be easily destroyed.

A generational curse stems from a lack of knowledge. Continuing to teach the wrong thing perpetuates the outcome and yields a much worse result each time. To perpetuate the outcome is to be held accountable, and to be held responsible means that one becomes aware of their transgressions while the act(s) remain ongoing.

The results will always be the same unless someone chooses to use their God-given gift of freedom to think, control, and rule over their destiny. To gain knowledge is to be free from all curses that may result in any mental entrapment.

Common sense is the foundation of all humility; it makes a humble seed sprout into a seedling in time, and carries that same seed to great heights as a tree. Nevertheless, one thing remains the same. Despite the height of success the trunk, branches, and leaves reach, the root remains grounded, making it all possible. To leave the ground of humility is to be uprooted from the source of your main existence.

Humility, or common sense, enables excellent knowledge to soar to the heights, but through a humble nature, wisdom and understanding are gained as a prize in the inheritance of knowledge. Humility is what makes a wise man wiser, a great man greater, because even though he is high, he is grounded at the same time. Even a bird that flies the skies often knows that it must come down to its simple beginnings to maintain its nature to fly again.

The Great Ending is upon us, and many are strutting through the streets as if everything is fine. The cause of the end began within the home, where an autonomous relationship prevails. The results from the family heads perpetuate an imbalance that is passed down to the entire bodily unit (offspring).

Many have failed and continue to fail to follow the example set by our original parents, King Alpha and Queen Omega. They choose to maintain perfect order and stability by becoming balanced through the Will of the Great One. They were both established as rulers of ideal equity, neither having self-rule over the other, yet interdependent. The sun and the moon are never in disarray because each understands the importance of its role and the need for the other.

The Mystery Behind Life, Death and Resurrection

When there is autonomy within a relationship, the right hand opposes the left hand, and division arises within a unit that is supposed to be whole. If the right hand were to be cut off, the entire body would be maimed because part of it is lost forever. This is the point at which an offspring must choose between its parents, and it marks the beginning of imbalance. When both parents oppose each other, the child suffers because there are two conflicting teachings from both parents.

Favouritism is a telltale sign of imbalance, not only within the home but in nature itself. We complain when the sun is too hot, and we pray for the rain, but when the rain falls too much, we pray for the sun. In times like those, we show favour to one side, bringing down the other, yet we are the ones causing the imbalances. Recognising such imbalances serves as a warning, as it clearly shows that we are doing or perpetuating something wrong or harmful to our existence.

Arguments are signs that balance is being breached and that it needs to be restored. Illnesses are signs that the body needs to be balanced and restored because its health has been breached. The sun is becoming too hot, warning us of our own destruction. Natural phenomena such as hurricanes, earthquakes, and tsunamis warn us of our perpetuated imbalances. When the Earth cries for help against the human destroyers, nature responds with natural disasters as an aid. After all, the Earth is the child of the Holy Trinity.

The constant cataclysms are not negative but are simply scolding, intended to teach us who is actually in charge. Moreover, they make us aware of our lack of control over the destruction we trigger through our constant acts of imbalance. All these natural disasters are just warnings signalling the End of a destructive race of people who are in control of the world, but also of their own genocide. It is analogous to antivirus software for computer networks, which is designed to eradicate harmful viruses.

A house that is kept well will always last longer than one that is left abandoned. Taking care of your home is to be well known by it, as you become a necessity to its standing in uprightness, a significant part of the strength it possesses. You would not have a wooden house and light a fireside within. You would then become a threat to your dwelling. It is the same with the Earth; we have now become a threat to it, and so many are no longer identifiable as part of it. We are barely taking care of our bodily abode, and the End of many is soon upon us. Global Warming is like setting a house made of highly flammable materials on fire.

As a result of our perpetuation of an imbalanced state, the End is becoming increasingly imminent as we become more detached from the Spiritual connection of all things. The sun and the moon warn us, through the instability of the seasons, that the Great Divine is becoming distant, even though it is nearby. The cycles are also responsible for destruction.

We are no longer looking up to our true parents, King Alpha and Queen Omega, and in doing so, we are interfering with the course of nature. It is we who are showing the Holy Trinity that we have chosen death over eternal bliss. It is we who are deeming ourselves unworthy and unfit for continued existence. Having understood the concept of Time, one ought to know that the end is already

The Mystery Behind Life, Death and Resurrection

here. We are living at the End of a terrible cycle; Judgment Day has already begun, and many know it not.

Many honestly don't understand how blessed we are. We were granted dominion over a force far greater than us, one that is beyond the flesh. The Holy Trinity submitted itself to the service of man in the same way most parents sacrifice their lives for the well-being of their offspring. We were given authority over eternal entities as a gift. We were given all that we would ever need to fulfil our birthright, achieve our highest possible level of superhumanism, and exist eternally.

To lack knowledge is to be utterly destroyed physically, eternally condemned spiritually, and rendered non-existent for eternity. Many continue to abuse the temporary power granted unto us, and many suppress the Great Divine. Neither the body nor the spirit is fighting for continued existence. The world is without end, and the Spirit of the Great Divine One could never die; they have already accomplished much since the Beginning. It is our human consciousness; our human identity is at stake.

It all comes down to the decisions or choices we make, as we don't have much more time. We came here as a number, only to be given further identification. Being granted the authority to make choices can have both benefits and drawbacks. It could maintain a balanced or imbalanced state, depending on how the Holy Power gained is used. To utilise the Power of balance in the right way is to become one with the Spirit and further become a part of that which is eternal at the highest order of all existence.

To not utilise the Power of balance is to detach oneself from the root of all existence. To become detached from the Spirit is to become the embodiment of destruction, from which the wild animals have become a threat unto us, as we have become a threat unto them. This is because the higher levels of the Spirit no longer connect with us. To become one with nature is to become associated with all things, and wild creatures would treat you as the ground they lay upon. One may now understand why the lions in the den did not eat Daniel.

We no longer communicate with the trees, yet we continue to destroy ourselves by eradicating them. We tend to lose our sense of truth, yet retain a sound belief in lies. Thus, we continue to deceive ourselves as we lose connection with the primary source of All Things. We are no longer in tune with nature, which knows not its children of the Earth; we are now seen as threats. We are not seen as inhabitants but as invaders; we are alienating ourselves within our own abode.

The cycles that were once in perfect harmony, serving a balance provided by nature itself, are now working in perfect harmony, even though we orchestrated our own demise by offsetting our balance, even that of nature.

This is why there would be famine and pestilence, rumours of wars, the spread of plagues, sicknesses and diseases, earthquakes in diverse places, unprecedented hurricanes (such as Patricia in 2015), tsunamis and volcanic eruptions. Global Warming is imminent, as humanity would be its own destroyer. Atomic warfare and autonomy rule cannot stop the changes of time in "The Now."

The sun's energy is entering in much greater amounts due to the destruction of the ozone layer and even the Earth's magnetic field.

The Sun isn't getting hotter because it isn't hot at all; our planet is becoming unbearable because it is designed to operate as a microwave, as the human body thrives on heat.

Fire will soon cover the heavens due to the accelerated greenhouse effect, in which trapped gases continue to trap heat, making the planet hotter as less heat is radiated back into space.

It was written in 2 Peter 3:10-12 (KJV) that the heavens shall be on fire, and the elements shall melt with fervent heat and be dissolved, and the earth also, and the works that are therein, shall be burned up.

A prophecy that is given can be fulfilled or prevented because it is based on a choice. To become detached from the Spirit is to genuinely believe that prophecies that were written and set in stone have to be fulfilled. It is intended as a warning and not to be taken out of context by a left-leaning thinker who knows nothing about cultivating high spirituality. It is like people who take parables and metaphorical statements literally, thinking they mean precisely what they state. It is we who gave and were given prophecies so that we could save ourselves from our actions or ways of imbalance that only lead to destruction.

Our destinies are not set in stone but are written as we go; we have the choice to keep them fixed or make them flexible. As for the past generations who have paved the way, we praise our foreparents, our ancestors, for their sustained efforts to help protect this planet. One day, the future generation will praise our efforts and call us great, just as we do for those who are here now and those who were before us.

Tevin C. R. Dubé

Therefore, it is my privilege to praise you, the future generation, even the unborn, who may carry on the mantle of truth until this world returns to a state of paradise once more, as it was in the beginning. The end of a horrible cycle is at its precipice; its end is inevitable, and so is the start of a new beginning, a new cycle of redemption and salvation for the fallen race of Atom.

17
Of Concerning Hell

To be a part of Heaven itself is for those who know themselves and overstand their true purpose. Even though the Earth is within heaven and we are part of the Earth within heaven, that doesn't necessarily mean we become one with heaven itself. Heaven is a birthright, and only those who are born of heaven can return to heaven.

As a result of such, the Messiah said unto Nicodemus, *"Verily, verily, I say unto thee, except a man be born again, he cannot see the kingdom of God* [John 3:3 KJV]. *"Verily, verily, I say unto thee, except a man be born of water and the spirit, he cannot enter into the kingdom of God. That which is born of the flesh is flesh; and that which is born of spirit is spirit. Marvel not that I said unto thee, Ye must be born again. The wind bloweth where it listeth, and thou hearest the sound thereof, but canst not tell whence it cometh, and whither it goeth: so is every one that is born of the spirit."* [John 3:5-8 KJV]

In other words, Melanin is the Spirit of the Universe and is the Order in which Heaven came into being. Melanin is the order in which human nature came into existence. To be born of the Spirit of Melanin, in which is heaven, is to be able to return unto the rightful birthplace from whence one came, but through the second birth through the cosmic vagina of the Pineal Doorway and not necessarily through physical water baptism.

Hence, one may now fully understand the scripture, *"Not everyone that saith unto me, Lord, Lord, shall enter into the kingdom of heaven; but he that doeth the will of the Father which is in heaven. Many will say to me in that day, Lord, Lord, have we not prophesied in thy name? and in thy name have we cast out devils? And in thy name have many wonderful works? And then will I profess unto them, I never knew you: depart from me, ye that work iniquity."* [Mathew 7:21-23 KJV]

Earth is merely a trinket in our possession because the vast Universe is our true inheritance. To fight over the Earth is like someone who owns an entire gold chain but focuses solely on one link, claiming that link as their own. It is like owning a T-shirt and claiming that a single thread hanging belongs unto thee, notwithstanding that the entire jersey belongs unto thee.

Heaven, we came from, so it is to Heaven we shall return. We are one with the Most High Divine. Our minds are one with the Universal Mind of the Great Divine. Our bodily vessels are an inheritance of the Earth and one with it; our breath is one with the Air, and our Spirits are one with the entire Cosmic Being. That is, the Great Divine Darkness. Some say that we are humans having a Spiritual experience, but nay, we are Spirits having a human

The Mystery Behind Life, Death and Resurrection

experience. We are the Great Galactic travellers; we are the Holy Celestial Beings. For Heaven is where we truly belong, so please 'Know Thyself.'

In basic science, whether in cosmology or astronomy, one is initially taught that our solar system contains the Sun, which is by far the most significant body, much larger than Jupiter. However, the Sun is not considered a planet but rather a star because of its nature.

The original definition of Lucifer is the 'Morning Star', Bringer of Light, Light Bearer, or A Shining One. All those glittering stars that can be clearly seen at night are only visible to the naked human eye because of the darkness of the night. Lucifer is still the morning star, or the 'Sun' of the morning, and is in no wise Satan or the Devil. It is still the only star that can be seen during the day, as it is that which makes the mortal day possible, beginning in the morning.

People who tend to 'curse Lucifer', calling him Satan, are cursing your Original Father, the One who holds the seeds of physical Creation. Lucifer was truly present in the Beginnings of Man's Creation and is not any Satan, because Lucifer is none other than the Original King Alpha, the first Male principle of Nature Atom and of the flesh Adam. Lucifer is not simply the 'Son of the morning' but is, in fact, the 'Sun of the morning'—and because of this, all Life is made possible upon the face of the Earth.

As a result of the Greco-European nature, left-brain or left-sided thinkers believed that Lucifer is Satan, the Lord of the underworld. His domains are the place or region of hell, or Patala, a fiery dwelling of pain and torture for the unsaved soul.

This is not so for us, because we were and are continuously programmed under a 'slave system' to believe in the ways of left-brain thinkers, psychologically training our minds to such a belief. Thus, we are mentally manipulated as we go against our nature, being right-sided thinkers who conform to ways opposed to ours. What we have here is a sound sleep of death and the inability to control one's own vehicle of travel.

This world is, in fact, the underworld, in which dominion was given to the sun from the beginning of physical Creation, along with the moon, or King Alpha and Queen Omega, respectively. Lucifer is, in fact, the ruler of this domain, but is not the Devil; he remains the provider of sustainable living for Humans.

They say that left-handed people owe the Devil, but it is a fact that left-handed people are naturally right-handed thinkers. The same can be said for artists, musicians and writers.

The reason Lucifer (the sun) was considered Satan by Greco-Europeans was the absence of Melanin or pigmentation. The sun's heat would burn them up, as they were confined to living most of their daily lives in caves or the lower parts of the Earth, or Patala, where they hid from Lucifer's glorious light. It is not so for us, as we are the children of the sun, and there was no need for us to believe in any Devil that is a bringer of fire, in that we are already in a fiery furnace of Hell.

"Their arrogance is but skin deep and an assumption that has no foundation in morals or in law. They have sprung from the same family tree of obscurity as we have; their history is as rude in its primitiveness as ours; their ancestors ran wild and naked, lived in caves and in the branches of trees, like monkeys, as ours; they

made human sacrifices, ate the flesh of their own dead and the raw meat of wild beasts for centuries even as they accuse us of doing; their cannibalism was more prolonged than ours; when we were embracing the arts and sciences on the banks of the Nile their ancestors were still drinking blood and eating out of skulls of their conquered dead; when our civilization had reached the noonday of progress they were still running naked and sleeping in holes and caves with rats, bats and other insects and animals. After we had already unfathomed the mysteries of stars and reduced the heavenly constellations to minute and regular calculus, they were still backwoodsmen, living in ignorance and blatant darkness.

The world today owes us the benefits of civilisation. They stole our arts and sciences from Africa. Then why should we be ashamed of ourselves? Their MODERN IMPROVEMENTS are but DUPLICATES of a grander civilization that we reflected thousands of years ago, without the advantage of what is buried and still hidden, to be resurrected and reintroduced by the intelligence of our generation and our prosperity. Why should we be discouraged because somebody laughs at us today? Who to tell what tomorrow will bring forth? Did they not laugh at Moses, Christ and Mohammed? Was there not a Carthage, Greece and Rome? We see and have changes every day, so pray, work, be steadfast and be not dismayed.

As the Jew is held together by his RELIGION, the white races by the assumption and the unwritten law of SUPERIORITY, and the Mongolian by the precious tie of BLOOD, so likewise the Negro must be united in one GRAND RACIAL HIERARCHY. Our UNION MUST KNOW NO CLIME, BOUNDARY, or NATIONALITY. Like the great Church of Rome, Negroes the world over MUST PRACTICE

Tevin C. R. Dubé

ONE FAITH, that of CONFIDENCE IN THEMSELVES with ONE GOD! ONE AIM! ONE DESTINY! Let no religious scruples, no political machination divide us, but let us hold together under the climes and in every country, making among ourselves a Racial Empire upon which, 'the sun shall never set'." – Marcus Garvey [Selected Writings and Speeches of Marcus Garvey, edited by Bob Blaisdell, pg. 185]

Those who are of a high-Melanin content, when we call Lucifer Satan, we are cursing our true Father, and we are significantly punished because we continue to perpetuate our imbalances by not embracing our nature. That serpent, considered the deceiver of Man, is actually the good guy, as it is we as 'Man'. It is that of our spinal cord.

When we keep fuelling our fears with something that doesn't exist, a lack of knowledge, which is the foundation of the world, we are greatly destroyed. Think about it. Because of Melanin, one could remain in the sun all day while working. Slavery only worked for so long because we not only had the ideal skin type but also because our Melanin was extensively studied, and we allowed ourselves to be conquered by falling asleep, choosing not to know ourselves as a result of instilled fear.

Other races quickly failed and were subjected to genocide through overwork, could not withstand diseases and weather conditions, nor the new mental conformities of Life that were being programmed and given. 'Africans' were genetically built to withstand all strains; we eat the sun, literally, just as the leaves of trees do through the process of photosynthesis. Because of our pigmented skin, we absorb the sun's rays, enabling our bodies to produce vitamin D. Hence, we need not eat or drink any dairy products, because dairy produces Vitamin D in those of a melanin-recessive nature, as with Caucasians. Still, unto us it is an act of becoming anti-melanin.

One melanin pigment can withstand temperatures of 1225°f. Skin cancer from heat and radiation is significantly decreased; it is not the same for Caucasians and others with low amounts or no melanin on the skin. It is a fact that people with high melanin would always survive because this planet needs us to remain in existence.

Racial warfare is solely for the destruction of the one who is prejudiced. I do support White Supremacy, just like Marcus Garvey, because melanated people were made to survive independently and were doing so for millions of years before mankind existed, and will continue to do so afterwards. To keep fighting and killing us is only to destroy yourselves and your kind forever. We were made to adapt and conform to any state of subjection and oppression, and to conquer triumphantly in the end. It is inevitably ordained by the Laws of Nature and forever backed by the entire Universe.

In Hindu cosmology, Patala is the lowest realm in heaven. This is further evidenced by the team of scientists led by Brent Tully at the University of Hawaii. Within the Supercluster Laniakea, our galaxy lies on the outskirts, at the edge of a structure containing thousands of other galaxies. In Sanskrit, Patala is described as the lowest realm in which lower beings, such as Nagas (or snake people), vetalas, and asuras, dwell.

Tevin C. R. Dubé

We are already in hell because here is the only place where the illusion of pain is actually felt. The experience of Earthly Life is just as portrayed in the movie 'The Matrix.' This realm is an illusion, a projection of the Universal Mind, through which we are plugged in via the intricate network of Melanin, making the experience feel so real. Melanin is responsible for creating.

It is like the movie 'Inception'; we are now within a dream. Some are consciously aware, whilst others are consciously unaware. However, within this dream of Life, one can venture further into it, and one can become trapped if one is not able to come back out in time. In Life, we are dreaming, and the illusions associated with it can be delved into in a perpetual way, in which many have, are still doing, and will continue to lose themselves if they continue to postpone the search for actual knowledge about Knowing Thyself.

Pigmented people, Coloured People, this Life of Physical Existence is proof that we are truly asleep. You want to be truly awakened? Then always be prepared and willing to die. Death of the flesh is inevitable; it was designed to free us if we were ever caught in a perpetuating trap.

As a result of Melanin, the illusion of sight becomes real, taste is given, and the sense of touch is made possible, as all things physical are vibrations of atoms, each of which is not solid. The flesh is made possible because of Melanin; the illusions of pain and death have also been accepted as real. In fact, the entire fabric of our reality is considered as real as can be, but is in fact an act of surrealism by our true Universal Nature. Nothing in this realm truly exists.

The Mystery Behind Life, Death and Resurrection

Patala, or Earth, even the realm of physicality, is the actual hell for those who choose not to know themselves and are caught within the veil of this profound illusion. This existence is itself a dream, and we must become aware to awaken from our current comatose state. If not, one would constantly have to endure the fears of Life and Decay, as the Buddha mentions in the Dhammapada.

This realm is so tricky that it can be attested to as the Greatest Challenge the Most High Being has ever experienced. We have entered the realm of Patala, or Hell, as many of us have, so that we can become guides and motivators for one another. We are all here to establish Heaven on Earth, from whence it was mentioned within the Bible that God would create a kingdom for Satan and his legions to have dominion over.

In the Book of Enoch, Enoch, upon his departure to meet God, described the realm of hell as the lower realms of heaven as he travelled through the sky.

This is a realm in which the lower beings dwell, and in which Lucifer, the Sun, is made ruler over its provinces. This peculiar realm is where Gods can become trapped. True angels, considered fallen, forgot how to fly again because of a lack of knowledge.

Alkebulanites, or anyone of the Nature of Melanin, would be constantly reborn or reincarnated over many lifetimes right here, suffering the cycle of Life and Death. One would continually have to live through the tortures of fear, only to restart afresh from the state of a baby, losing all consciousness of one's past existence, yet inheriting all through the Knowledge of Self, so that one could truly free oneself. From whence the parable, "You can lead a horse to water but cannot force it to drink," becomes factual, as it is you who alone can truly save yourself.

One would constantly have to endure the illusion's enormity of a heavy conscience, feel pain of all degrees, and suffer significant sicknesses and illnesses, which also include greed, ego, and prejudice. This is the only place where the truth is contorted and can be challenging to piece together if you don't know that you are the key to all things, because the truth could never be destroyed.

Melanin is a blessing that will forever remain dominant and never recessive. Not even 'admixture' can alter its dominance. O rise, ye people of the Most High Divine, and take your rightful stand. The time is at hand; the time is 'Now'.

Artificial intelligence and electronics can only distract so many for so long from nature's naturalness. Still, through the natural energies of our Melanated skins, as the new cycle approaches, those who are imprisoned shall be set free, mentally, spiritually, physically and emotionally. The anointing of feeding your mind the knowledge of truth shall only make you fatter and fatter until the yokes around our necks are broken through proper feeding. As the nature of our sun changes, we will soon be able to fly again. Each melanin granule is a tiny feather, and when energised by the ankh of levitation, gods were given the power of flight. [The Ankh: African Origin of Electromagnetism by Nur Ankh Amen]

Melanin granules function as tiny, primitive eyes, forming a vast neural network that absorbs and decodes electromagnetic waves. Your lack of knowing thyself is what you would greatly suffer, because you would only see Life from a one-sided, one-tracked mind through anti-melanin or melanin-recessive beings. As a result, you would struggle to cultivate proper awareness and would not be able to reach your perfect state. You would repeat this cycle of Life and Death 9000 times until you finally get it right. The road to perfection begins here. If one does it right this once, it doesn't have to be repeated, but it is on to the next one—the level of Higher Existence.

Think about it. If you have only one Life to live, why are many people often tired or fed up with Life? It is so because this Life is not new unto either of us, given the content of the Melanin we possess. Life is not new unto us who are of true human nature, but to that of the new body which is now being possessed by it, because each is unique and distinctive every time. Because of Melanin, we have experienced and conquered all things.

Your melanin is a gift, and because of it, you can access the Pineal Gateway within the mind, which is always open, forever active and dominant, and never yet calcified or permanently closed off within thee. It is as helpless for any other race to save us as it is for them to save themselves truly. We are the light of our souls and the eternal light of the world, even though our embodiment is that of Divine Darkness. Melanin is the result of absorbing all colours, and from the infinite Darkness, Light is made possible.

It is we who alone can save ourselves from physical extinction, yet we are eternally everlasting spiritually. Being spiritual is our true nature. We are the Light of the world and the Saviours of all Mankind. If we are all led to genocide, we would still forever exist, but this world would be no more. We are still the suppliers of Melanin on Earth; we are the single most precious commodity required for the existence of all Life and Life forms. It is we who bring spirituality wherever we go because we are spirits having a human experience.

This vessel is very much a prison unto the Most High, but this temple was designed to be only temporal, for it cannot keep our true selves locked away forever. Hence, through death, Christ was given the keys to hell, in which he was able to free the souls of the imprisoned. He possessed the power of Melanin, and all things were given to him by his true Father, who is within heaven. "Destroy this temple, and in three days I will raise it." [John 2:19 KJV] This is the same time in which a sperm begins the reconstruction of a brand new temple unto the Most High.

This vessel is meant to be a living sacrifice for the sake of Man's continued existence. Hence, the reason the Messiah said he was a lamb of ultimate sacrifice was that he came into the world to carry out the will of the Most Divine. Out of Love, he was said to have laid down his life for his friends.

Death is nothing to be feared at all, especially for us, for we are the help that came. Hence, the Messiah was sent unto the twelve Tribes of Judah with the Knowledge of Self, as it is the key unto Salvation. To reject our assistance through continuous regimes to extinguish us is to hurt your existence forever. Death of all flesh is inevitable, but to be born again is through the inheritance of Melanin.

Let us all live this Life well, and you don't need to live another. Contented is the happiest person in this Life, because the love of this world would not become the perpetual imprisonment that has held captive the slaves of many. Such a person would be thoroughly satisfied at every point of this journey of existence and would be bound for an eternity of happiness in this existence and the ones to come thereafter. So, having little to no attachment within this illusory sphere is to maintain a free mind by the upkeep of a free spirit, which would allow the state of transition or the acceptance of change to be embraced at all times.

The Buddha was said to have left his wife and son in pursuit of Nirvana. To be truly free, one must have no significant attachment to the flesh, for it is forever short-lived, but dwelling upon it is what keeps many attached to this wretched form of existence.

By accomplishing this, you would be free to become part of a much greater and glorious existence. Hence, it is easier for a camel to walk through the eye of a needle than for a poor man who is still physically rich but very much attached to the illusion of material possessions and vanity, and to the physical realm itself.

During the transition stage, each came individually, so returning requires the same principles. You went without a single possession, not even the flesh, but with the forces of Melanin. Melanin is all that was needed to arrive, and it is solely that which is required to return. That eye of the needle is your Third Eye. To enter through that Gate of Heaven, you cannot be attached to the physical, much less to material possessions. The only thing that entered freely, no matter the enormity, was truthful knowledge of all things—pure spirituality. The Most High Supreme entered this realm, All-knowing, so to leave, one must be fully aware of the Great Force that is within.

As much as Melanin is a divine blessing, it can also become a divine curse through sheer lack of knowledge. Used, it can set one free eternally, or, misused, it can leave one eternally trapped in a never-ending cycle. The only difference is that Melanin is the only thing that could break the cycle or perpetuate it. We are the Beginning and the Ending of all physical Existence. We are the creators of this and all other realities here, because they are all projections of our thoughts; we are the creators of our reality.

Embrace yourselves, all ye true citizens of the Earth. Behold the Great Divine Darkness and rejoice, for Melanin is the natural Chemical Key to your freedom. Together, in the oneness of peace with ourselves first, and then with all our fellow men, we can save all of humanity. If we don't come together on the same page, many more will have to suffer, and many more will have to die. When shall we open our eyes and see? Awake, ye sleeping giants, from your slumber, and let thy good will be done on earth as it is already within your heavens. This is the cry and laughter of the Most Divine One unto all Alive.

18
The Reward of Humility

The Tree: At the beginning of Creation, after the heavens were created, the Earth was fashioned and formed, and the waters were divided, giving way for dry land. From the ground came forth the first living things: Grass, herb-yielding seeds, and the tree yielding fruits after its kind and whose seed was after its kind. [Gen 1:11-12 KJV]

A tree is the embodiment of humility. It has never strayed from its original purpose, as its roots are loyalty. The job it performs is of utmost importance, as its functions are a key element of all physical existence. It regenerates the single most precious commodity vital to the beginning of all living things. It harbours the Breath of Life that was given in abundance from the Most Divine Entity that is responsible for all Existence.

Simple, yet it stands, never exalting itself above all things despite the great duty it was tasked with and has continuously executed, never failing once. Without it, we would suffocate and die.

Tevin C. R. Dubé

It is axiomatic to the resilience of a tree, for its nature is very much providential. It transforms death into the regeneration of life by absorbing carbon dioxide and releasing oxygen. We cut them down without divine permission, poison, burn, and destroy them without thought or consideration, yet still exonerate ourselves. Faithful unto us, it has yet remained, even though the exorbitant ways of many are yet still evident unto it.

The tree is the ultimate example of humility on Earth. It remains forever humble in its very existence. It has endured much, yet it still stands tall. The tree knows its worth and knows itself. It sprang from the humblest beginnings to a grand nature of mystical divinities. It truly embodies a love that is Universal by Nature.

The tree has been the oldest living thing to first grace the face of the Earth, and as it was in the beginning, so shall it be in the end. The herbs are the healing of the nation [Revelation 22:2 KJV]. The tree, in itself, has always been the longest-living thing, even knowing the mysteries of man. They, too, bear witness to the origins of Life that took on the appearance of flesh.

The tree faced all earthly epidemics, witnessed human suffering in all its degrees, and withstood the dire predicaments of mass destruction. It suffered greatly but endured triumphantly in the end. It knows all things and can teach of great mysteries, yet its humility is often overlooked because many have become distanced from it. After six years, the Buddha purportedly achieved enlightenment through intense meditation under a Tree.

This is the valid reward of humility. Being loyal to your roots, the origins of all truths, is the foundation of humility. Knowing one's true purpose is to take deep root and grow stronger and stronger the deeper you penetrate. The valid reward of humility is to exist forever and to be eternally enlightened infinitely. One would forever become a perpetuating event, an everlasting Entity. There is truly never an ending unto thee, for every ending is the symbolic signal of a newer, much more improved and better beginning.

To end old is to begin anew and afresh, as a seed to a tree and as a tree to its seed.

Tevin C. R. Dubé

The Reverse

Night is Day and Day is Night!

We are living in the reverse. We are the reverse. We are all living on the opposite side of the Universe. The realm of 'All' physicality is within the bounds of the entire Universe. The Universe is the mirror reflection of The Great Beyond. The Physical Realm is the reverse of the principle of the Great Divine Being. To be a human being is to represent the outer limitations of the Most High Divine but still inwardly contain its infinite Nature. Mortal men are a reversed version of 'God-Infinite' being 'God-Finite Infinitely. The entire Universe is the outer limit of The Great Beyond because it is physically infinite, undergoing constant change, re-correcting and reconstructing itself, unlike The Great Beyond, which is never submissive to Time and Change.

The Centre Point of the entire Universe and all of Creation is Love. To be filled with the Order of Love fervently is to become One with the whole Universe and to be a part of The Great Beyond, which is infinite beyond the Universe as a whole.

The Mystery Behind Life, Death and Resurrection

The Centre Point of Creation, or the Origination of All Things, is a condensed 'Black Dot', from a humanoid point of view. From this somewhat Darkened Centre Point emanates the very Sound of Creation. It is the high-frequency resolution of the sound "OM." From this Grand Vibration of Creation, a series of triangular shapes perpetually forms. This Holy Sound takes on the very form of a tetrahedron, a four-faced triangle, as we can see today in the pyramids built by the ancient Egyptians. This formation is the same connection point of the Holy Trinity, in which Its untamed Forces meet to become One, yet are always perfectly stabilised and balanced by the Great Centre Point connection of all Creation.

To first understand the Universe and all that is within it is to know thyself. To then understand how the entire Universe came into existence is to be aligned with the Centre Point of all Existence. To understand this ineffable and illustrious Centre Point is to know the Force of Melanin. This hallowed Centre Point is the single most potent force known throughout the entire Universe and beyond. It could never truly be destroyed. This is the magnified power of the Most High Supreme Being. It is the only Force that can be Everything all at once.

The Force of Melanin is invisible yet visible. It is intangible yet tangible. While it is high, it is simultaneously low; even though it remains below, it is above. It is a gas that can liquefy, solidify, and crystallise simultaneously. This is the great All in All existence of the Most High Supreme Being. Melanin is the One true Force that is Omnipresent, Omnipotent and Omniscient.

The entire Universe and that which lies beyond the Great Beyond are filled with the concentrated and indestructible Force of Melanin. The highest known pigmentation in man appears as the 'taught' colours known as Blue/Black. No one can truly explain precisely what a colour is. Who could truly define what is blue or what is green unless they are in its presence to show precisely what it is? In the truest sense, it is unto the likeness of water, which is colourless yet still contains the essence of all colours, just as water contains the very essence for a prolonged physical existence.

To prove that the entire Universe consists of the Highest Order of Melanin is to distinguish the difference within the heavens during the carnal version of the Night and Day. At sunrise, it takes on the appearance of blue, and at nightfall, it predominantly takes on the appearance of darkness or the colour 'black', as depicted by the human sense of sight.

At least this is what is believed to be accurate and honest in the general human mindset, which is of a reversed principle. Seeing does not always mean believing; what goes up doesn't necessarily come down; and what goes around does not always come back around, but what ensues is undoubtedly some form of balance. What is bounded by earth is liberated by heaven, and what is released from heaven is temporarily bounded by earth.

We are a temporal existence within a reversed reality because we are the opposing factor to our most valid form of existence. But what makes us infinite, even though we are individually temporal, is the process of procreation. The Infinite Powers of the Universe take on the highest concentration of Melanin 'Blue/Black' in its visual picturesque unto the naked human eyes. However, the Universe is unto the likeness of a jaded emerald stone or a mighty diamond, crafted and dimensionally cut to perfection, never radiating the same colour twice infinitely.

It is the same way that no two snowflakes are ever the same; neither are any two grains of sea sand on all beaches, nor any two human fingerprints, blood types, hair follicles, and so much more. They are never the same and will never be the same.

Therefore, by the eternal Laws of Nature itself, those that are natural by nature are, by fact, more genetically dominant. A forced-ripe mango will share the same roots of a tree, but when its time comes to an end, it is never a good fruit, nor can its seed ever germinate. It is the same with a grafted tree; it may bear fruit, but the seed of its fruit could never lead to a continuous state of fruition. That tree would live its time, and after that, it ceases to exist.

Hence, it is a proven fact that the Order of Melanin would eternally be the most superior force and will ever exist. However, with respect to the entire human population, the dominant species would always be those blessed by the Universal Order of Mel-chis'-e-dec or the Spirit of the Most High Divine. This is the Word of Nature and has been proven axiomatic by Mendel's Law of the traits of dominant and recessive alleles, found not only in peas but also in the genetics of man and mankind.

As a result of the reversed nature of the entire human vessel, and, by extension, of the eyes and the inducement of visual impact upon the perception of our thoughts and what we were taught to believe, the now-recorded human experience of physical existence is literally made to be back-to-front. What we consider as 'white' is actually the real appearance of 'black', and what is considered 'black' is actually 'pure' in nature. Melanin is the colourless colour, making it the purest, as it contains all other colours. Being similar to water, it is a clear Liquid Light that literally binds and keeps all physical matter together.

So, in reality, the darker your complexion appears to the human eye, the purer and brighter your spiritual light shines. This Liquid Light, responsible for All Existence, is permeated through the Centre Point, or Cosmic Vagina, upon deep penetration from the Great Beyond, giving birth to the entire Universe; and it is responsible for binding together all the fabrics of physicality. It is the Creation and Evolution of Atoms. It is the very subatomic particles of electrons, protons and neutrons that make up an atom, and that which is within each particle infinitely. It then fuels our Sun, and the Sun fuels us through its rays, as our Melanin-enriched nature transmutes them into vitamin D upon contact with our skin and coiled hair. It is similar to photosynthesis, which occurs in plant leaves, in that we actually consume the Sun's rays.

Amen: A Great Light within Divine Darkness is Melanin. Its brightness is only clearly visible at night, because it is a revealing light of the spirit, yet perceived as darkness unto humanity; it only appears to be 'blue' because of the darkness of day, which is still perceived as light unto men. However, the Great Light of Amen that exists within the Divine Darkness (daylight) is any being that has the gift of pigmentation, with the pure content of Melanin within and without. It doesn't matter if you are 'black', 'brown', 'blue', 'red', 'purple' or even 'yellow.'

To be pigmented is to be part of and one with the entire Universe, and by extension, aligned with all of Existence. Through the Forces of Melanin, this Liquid Light follows us wherever we may choose to go, and it is our Guide perpetually. Heaven is our true birthright, and Earth is a mere destination stop or a little detour in our Galactic travels. Even though our bodies are within the world, our minds are not of the earth.

Being human, to sleep physically is to partially awaken the spirit, except when in a state of lucid dreaming, which is literally being aware that you are dreaming whilst still physically asleep. To sleep physically requires the 'darkness of the night', which significantly influences the secretion of Melatonin, which in turn is responsible for sleep, a temporary state of physical immobility. However, when asleep during the day, the eyelids mimic the night when closed, tricking the brain; the rest is never as fulfilling, as one often remains awake, feeling enervated.

The Nighttime for the flesh is actually Daytime for the spirit, because the Melanin of the Universe is truly the brightest light there is. That is why the light seen by the eyes cannot be penetrated by what is perceived to be a 'black hole' by humans, because it is said to be a light-bending agent. It is, in fact, the brightness of this so-called 'black hole' that renders the darkness of man's perceived thoughts of light invisible. These tunnels of Light are a medium through which only Spiritual Beings can access the entire Universe.

Understand that the natural human eyes will never see these things unless they are first perceived through the Third Eye Vision.

The brightness of the night is blinding to the human eye, for it will always appear dark at first until one realises that you truly never see with one's eyes but rather with the mind. Hence, the eyes can still adjust to see a bit through the brightness, not the perceived darkness of the night, as much as they adjust to see through the darkness of the day that is considered light.

However, dawn for the flesh becomes night for the spirit, in the sense that the spirit becomes involuntarily active or somewhat dormant when the body is physically awakened. The light of the day is actually blinding or black to the spirit unless the Spiritual Foresight or Third Eye is fully activated, allowing you to see through this elaborate reversal of the illusion of multiplicities. It is to let your spirit be voluntarily active at all times, so it is never asleep.

We are not living to die—we are dying to live. This life is a living form of death, and death is a living form of life. Life is a living death because of a constant state of transition or change unto the physical, yet this leads unto another conscious state or form of existence unto the spiritual that is never yet subjected to cyclic changes or Time.

We are always subject to change physically because we are within the experience of a reversed reality. This reverse effect occurs not only in us but also in the Earth, our Galaxy, and, by extension, the Universe, as they continually evolve and grow.

The Universe is perfected through imperfections, as it is always in a constant state of correction and re-correction. It is never in a perfectly balanced state, as the Great Beyond, because it is perfectly imperfect, still leading it unto a perfect state of perfection. It always transitions through a deathlike state whenever it is in the physical, in which it is continually upgraded.

The Mystery Behind Life, Death and Resurrection

In one aspect, this can be considered the infinitely finite, or a lesser-great strength of the Most High Divine, which has made Itself low. The reason is that it is designed to be so, so that an untamed Force can be channelled and controlled for a period of time. Hence, the reason why the spinal cord is curved is that it breaks down the Universal Powers that flow downward from the crown of the head. It operates just like water rushing down from a mountain, but is channelled into canals and turbines, breaking down its untamed force, thus giving the pristine bliss of a pure and enjoyable waterfall. Yet it is still able to flow upwards in the same manner, just as the Great River Nile flows within the Continent of the first earthly dwellers that gave rise to all of humanity. It is Alkebulan, the Motherland or Garden of Eden, referred to today as modern-day 'Africa'.

Moreover, the Spirit of the Great Divine One knows no limit, for it is the very essence and embodiment of the Ego itself. Through the creation of the Universe, it intends to inherit a special kind of strength that can be obtained only through humility, by learning hands-on how to fully possess and understand the Power of Mind physically, to become the very perfection of being perfectly Balanced Itself. It is to be developed through personal experience, encompassing the causes and effects of a nature characterised by polarities.

So, apart from already being Almighty, the physical realm, and by extension humanity, was established to test the true power of creating something from nothing, as our very thoughts come from a place that is left unknown and unseen. Today, we have many languages, different ways of life, and so much more because we are Creator Beings tapping into the endless reservoir of All

Existence Itself. We are here to learn how to harness and control the untamed Forces of the entire Universe, but only for a temporal period of time individually, while collectively, as a chosen people, eternally, until it is all fully mastered.

The Centre Point of All Existence is the point that represents the State of Perfect Balance. It is the point that separates the immovable, unshakable and unchangeable Great Beyond from the ever-changing mirror reflection of the entire Universe. Still, it is the adjacent point that makes them one.

At that Great Centre Point, there is no right or wrong—only a perfect state of Zen. It is there that the actual state of heaven can be found, and there that you will find the tranquillity of the Most High Divine. No mere mortal instrument of flesh can ever discover such a thing unless it is found within you from the start.

So much more can be said, yet so little can be stated. This is the deep sleep of the Spirit of the Most High Divine Being, when in direct correlation with the flesh, as opposed to its truest side, which has never yet fallen asleep. To be fully awakened from this deep spiritual sleep requires that you remain asleep physically. Ha! It is pretty amusing—for even though I may be of sound mind, I am yet still likened unto a madman. We are literally living a dream, and many of us are scared to awake because we fear 'death' and have never ventured to be an analyst towards it.

It seems that I have broken the mystery of All Existence at its inception and have been granted permission to bring about a new revelation of the truthful Nature of the Great All in All. To truly see the Nature of the Most High Divine Being in its entirety, you must become that very Centre Point within your Universe by learning to balance and centre your every thought, regardless of what situation or circumstance may befall you. It is learning to adapt to the Order of Change, seeing the positive-negative and negative-positive relationship that leads to perfect balance.

This process allows the Lower Self to connect perfectly with the Higher Self, ushering in the Holy inheritance of the Mastered Self. Through the attainment of such profound power, you would be fully able to master the Power of Mind, from which All Things initially came, making you fully enlightened. This is the state of supra-consciousness; being fully aware of it all, long after one has transitioned from the plains of physical matter. This is the very place in which All Things initially began.

There are three main types of existence, and because of our freedom of choice, we choose among them. Whether the decision is direct or indirect, conscious or unconscious, it ultimately depends on the decisions we make individually and collectively.

One: You could choose to become One with the Spiritual Realm eternally. Two: You could choose to become One with all of physical existence, yet be constrained by an infinitely limited nature. Thirdly, you can choose to become one with the Great Centre Point of Balance eternally. To become One with the latter is the greatest of all; it is to become One with both the Spiritual and the Physical. To be part of such is to become One with Everything Infinitely; it is to become a part and One with the Mighty All in All.

The Beginning